2,000
SPORTS QUIPS
AND
QUOTES

GLENN LIEBMAN

GRAMERCY BOOKS
New York

To my wife, Kathy.
Your courage against impossible odds
is a source of strength for me.
You are my partner in crime,
my best friend,
and the greatest wife in the world.

This 1998 edition is published by Gramercy Books,®
an imprint of Random House Value Publishing, Inc.,
by arrangement with NTC/Contemporary Books,
4255 West Touhy Avenue, Chicago, Illinois 60646.

Gramercy Books® and colophon are registered trademarks of
Random House Value Publishing, Inc.

Random House
New York • Toronto • London • Sydney • Auckland
http://www.randomhouse.com/

Printed in the United States of America

Library of Congress Cataloging-in-Publication Data
Liebman, Glenn.
   [Sports shorts]
   2,000 sports quips and quotes / Glenn Liebman.
     p.   cm.
   Originally published: Sports shorts. Chicago: Contemporary Books,
c1993.
   ISBN 0-517-18934-8
   1. Sports—Quotations, maxims, etc.   2. Sports—Humor. I. Title.
II. Title: 2000 sports quips & quotes.   III. Title: Two thousand
sports quips and quotes.
[GV707.L53 1998]
796'.02'07—dc21
                                        97-48989
                                          CIP

Originally published as *Sports Shorts*

8 7 6 5 4 3 2 1

ACKNOWLEDGMENTS

Putting together this project has been both a labor of love and a love of labor. I have spent over five years working on this book. So many people have contributed in so many ways. Without trying to sound like a boring Academy Award winner, I would like to acknowledge many of these people.

I would first like to thank the librarians at the Baseball Hall of Fame library in Cooperstown, the New York State Library, and the library at my alma mater—The State University of New York at Albany. Thank you for having the periodicals and newspapers that helped put this book together. Thanks to the witty athletes and sportswriters who made this book possible (special thanks to Rocky Bridges, Abe Lemons, Pat Williams, and Frank Layden—the four all-time funniest men in sports).

I would also like to thank my wonderful agent, Philip Spitzer, who believed in this book from the start. Special thanks go to the people at Contemporary Books, who have given me the ultimate vote of confidence by publishing this book.

There are many other people who have made this book possible. Among them are John Kuenster, the editor of Baseball Digest, who gave me my first big break in 1988 when he published my first article. And countless others since then.

I would also like to thank New York Governor Mario Cuomo, a great and brilliant visionary who taught me that not only Don Quixotes can tilt at windmills but progressive pragmatists as well. Thanks to Elaine Ryan, who mixed compassion, intelligence, and humor better than anyone I've ever met. Thanks also to Robin Miller, who was a great secretary and a great friend. Thanks to Dick Starkey, who, to put it simply, is class personified. Thanks also to Woodie Fichette, whose legacy will never be forgotten.

Many other friends helped me along the way—people like the Hanfts (Big Louie), the Aglers, the Wallers, the Brandwins, the Wollners, the Sacks, the Mahers, the Merges, the Herbachs, the Vetrones, the Nolans, the Gayles, Victor and Gay, Joe Scarpa, Anna Leitner, Dr. Stephen Barr and staff, Marlene Lillis, Steve Keane (the Junior Wheel), Risa Pyles, Rosemarie Frisone, Drs. Abraham and Zeltner, Syndi Carney-Johnson, Mike Ferracane, and Dennis Kocyla.

I would especially like to say thanks for the contributions of four friends—Lou Roper (nice effort), David Wollner, Scott Sommer (Let's do lunch at La

Parisenne), and David Agler (25 years of friendship, and the truth is I really never liked you—always the kidder).

Thanks also go to some wonderful relatives, like Richard and Deanna Salpeter, Bernice Tannenbaum, Dan and Leanne, Bob and Marie Coll, Grandfather Coll, and especially my aunt Anna, my cousin Abbey, my "Uncle Hi" and great uncle Edward. All four of you are gone but never forgotten.

Thanks also to my three sisters-in-law—Laura, a world-class runner, Bridget, a world-class nutritionist and swimmer, and Deb, a world-class mother and attorney. Thanks also to the inspiration of my two gorgeous nieces—Aimee Kate (thanks to her mother, Kate) and Samantha Anne (who reminds me more of her grandmother every day). Thanks also to two of the funniest men I know—my brothers-in-law—Bob and Chris. Also, thanks to my future brother-in-law, Michael.

This book would not have been possible without the friendship and trust of my mother-in-law and father-in-law, Bill and Helen Coll—the two best in-laws in the world. Thanks also to Granny Murray, the grandmother I never had.

I would like to thank my father, Bernard Liebman, who taught me about generosity, courage, persistence, and fighting back against the odds. You have always served as an inspiration to me, and this book would not be possible without your lessons.

I would like to thank my brother Bennett, who

taught me to love sports. I'll always remember my first baseball game, when we actually saw Ed Kranepool in the flesh. Your contributions as a friend and confidant over the years will never be underestimated. You're the best.

I would especially like to thank my mother, Frieda Liebman, who, were she alive today, would have made this book a nationwide bestseller (even if she had to max out on a thousand credit cards to do it). I could never thank you for all you have done to make this book possible. Your love and friendship were unconditional. Your generosity, warmth, courage, and compassion are missed more with each passing day.

Finally, I would like to thank the academy (whoops—sorry). I would like to thank the gorgeous freckle-faced woman who for some reason married this balding windbag—my wife, Kathy. Your contributions to this book are too numerous to mention, but I'll try a few anyway. First, you encouraged me by letting me leave a good job to pursue a crazy dream. You have patiently put up with my leaving for libraries at 8:00 in the morning and coming home at 11:00 at night. Your love and friendship have sustained me through countless hours of research and hard work. You have helped me by patiently teaching me to use a computer and proofreading every word of this book. Marlene Dietrich once said it is the friends you can call at 4:00 A.M. that really count. I'm lucky to have my best friend around 24 hours of the day. Thank you for making this book possible.

INTRODUCTION

I had a friend when I was growing up who was Mr.
Front-runner. Name the team that just won the Super
Bowl, Stanley Cup, or World Series—chances are my
friend was that team's number-one fan. Most of us
sports fans are not front-runners. We live and die with
our favorite teams; mostly, we die. Despite the frustrations, sports isn't really tragedy. It's comedy. It's actually hilarious.

To point out the hilarity inherent in the sports
world, I put together this book which contains over
2,000 of the world's funniest one-liners.

Sure, there's Yogi and Casey, but there is also Pat
Williams, the general manager of the Orlando Magic,
who once said of heavyset center Stanley Roberts, "His
idea of a balanced meal is a Big Mac in each hand"; or
Bum Phillips, the former football coach who gives us
his two cents with his horse sense on the definition of

an expert: "He's just an ordinary fella away from home"; or Chuck Wepner, the boxer dubbed the Bayonne Bleeder, who said of his boxing career, "I was 6'1" when I started fighting, but with all the uppercuts I'm up to 6'5""; or the legendary Chi Chi Rodriguez, who recently said, "I'm getting so old, I don't even buy green bananas anymore."

My litmus test for including quotes was simple: they had to make me laugh. Putting this book together probably had me laughing harder than I have in my entire life (except when I watch Gregg Jefferies play second base).

I hope your enjoyment in reading the book matches the fun I had putting it together.

ACCESSORIES

✓ "Imagine having to tell a salesgirl that you're buying them for a wife who is 6'2" and weighs over 200 pounds."

Bill Robinson, on buying pantyhose for himself because of a muscle pull

ADVERTISING

✓ "I was offered a spot in an ad for neutering pets. Not exactly what I had in mind."

Steve Bedrosian, on offers received after winning the Cy Young Award

✓ "He's like the Midas Muffler man. You can pay now or pay later."

Mark Clayton, on Dan Marino's five-year, $25 million contract

1

"Jim Palmer's won 240 games, but it took a picture of him standing in his underwear to get nationally known."

Mike Flanagan

"He just keeps on going and going. He's like the Energizer rabbit."

Robert Parish, on the relentless play of 36-year-old Moses Malone

"The company should change its name to Mike."

Alvin Robertson, on all the ads Michael Jordan does for Nike

AGE

"If you don't live to get old, you die young."

Cool Papa Bell

"Now that I'm 20, it's downhill all the way, I suppose."

Bjorn Borg

"Tommy John is so old he uses Absorbine Senior."
Bob Costas

"As young as our team is, a lot of guys think we're in the hunt for a New Year's Day bowl game."
Rick Dalrymple, Dallas Cowboys public relations director, on fighting for a playoff spot with a young team

"Elvin is so old he had to use a jumper cable to get started last year."
Doug Dieken, on 14-year football veteran Elvin Bethea

"He is likely to be the only man in baseball history to collect a pension check and a salary check at the same time."
Eddie Fisher, on ageless veteran Hoyt Wilhelm, who played baseball well into his late 40s

"I knew it was Phil Niekro's. I found his teeth in my glove compartment."
Mike Flanagan, on a car the Blue Jays gave him

3

"Say, Satch, tell me, was Abraham Lincoln a crouch hitter?"

> *Lefty Gomez, discussing baseball in the old days with the legendary Satchel Paige*

"I don't mind turning 50. It's just at the beginning of the season I was 43."

> *Hank Greenwald, San Francisco Giants announcer, on turning 50 during a particularly bad Giants season*

"After 12 years the old butterflies come back. Well, I guess at my age you can call them moths."

> *Franco Harris, on playing for the Seattle Seahawks after 12 years with the Steelers*

"I'm waiting for the Senile Skin Games."

> *Bob Hope, on golfing at the age of 86*

"This is one you can tell your grandchildren about— tomorrow."

> *Rick Horton, on Jerry Reuss winning his 200th game at the age of 39*

"When I broke in, they didn't have bats—we just grabbed the branch off a tree."

Charlie Hough

"Good old Cy. Yeah, I think I pitched against him once in the Eastern League."

Tommy John, after tying the record of three errors in one inning, previously held by Cy Seymour back in 1898

"He's great to the old guys. He's got one trainer just to treat varicose veins."

Alex Karras, on George Allen

"I'm going to sell the 48-minute term insurance."

Johnny Kerr, former NBA player and insurance salesman, on the health of players in the NBA Old-Timers Game

"There goes Rick Monday. He and Manny Mota are so old that they were waiters at the Last Supper."

Tommy Lasorda

"The average age of our bench is deceased."

> Tommy Lasorda, on veterans Manny
> Mota and Vic Davalillo

"I hate homework."

> Maureen (Peanut) Louie, on why she
> became a tennis pro at the age of 18

"Swim, dance a little, go to Paris every August, and live within walking distance of two hospitals."

> Horatio Luro, horseracing trainer, ex-
> plaining the secret of his 80 years

"When Dr. Naismith put up the peach basket, Ray Meyer was holding the ladder."

> Al McGuire, discussing the 42-year
> coaching career of DePaul's Meyer

"It's just as well that I won because if Jennifer Capriati won, she couldn't drive it anyway."

> Martina Navratilova, after beating 14-
> year-old Capriati in a tournament and
> winning a car

✓"You know you're getting old when all the names in your black book have M.D. after them."
Arnold Palmer

✓"For aging boxers, first your legs go, then your re-flexes go, then your friends go."
Willie Pep

✓"The last time he leaned over to take the snap, he couldn't come out of the crouch."
Don Rickles, on longtime NFL veteran George Blanda

✓"I'm getting so old, I don't even buy green bananas anymore."
Chi Chi Rodriguez

✓"I've been here so long that when I got here the Dead Sea wasn't even sick."
Wimp Sanderson, after his 916th game as the Alabama basketball coach

✓"Getting my first Social Security check."
Gene Sarazen, golfing legend, who was asked what his greatest thrill was at the age of 72

7

"I told Hord [Masters chairman] I was getting too old to play, but he kept saying, 'Gene, they don't want to see you play; they just want to see if you're still alive.' "

Gene Sarazen, on his role as an honorary player in the Masters at the age of 90

"We've got so many kids on our roster, we're going to be the first team in football history with an equipment order for Pampers."

Ray Sewalt, Texas Christian University recruiting coordinator, on the youth of the team

"I may go on forever, because statistics say that few men die after the age of 100."

Amos Alonzo Stagg, celebrating his 100th birthday

"Old-timers' games, weekends, and airplane landings are alike. If you can walk away from them, they're successful."

Casey Stengel

"I'll never make the mistake of being 70 again."
Casey Stengel

"The trick is growing up without growing old."
Casey Stengel

"When you get old, everything is hurting. When I get up in the morning, it sounds like I'm making pop-corn."
Lawrence Taylor, on turning 33

"His nerves, his memory, and I can't remember the third thing."
Lee Trevino, on the three things that go on an aging golfer

"There are three ages: youth, adult, and 'Hey, you're looking good.'"
Leroy Walker, 1976 U.S. Olympic track coach

"Oscar Gamble is so old that when he broke into the majors he was still a Negro."
Stan Williams

"It was a rash statement, and I'd like to apologize to every vulture in the sky."

> *Mike Gottfried, former University of Pittsburgh coach, on saying that all sports agents were vultures*

"I treat agents like I treat drugs. I just say no."

> *Stan Kasten, Atlanta Hawks GM*

"A lot of people have told me I'm crazy for not using an agent, but I think I know my situation better than any agent could. Besides, I'm cheap."

> *Max Montoya, former Cincinnati Bengals guard, on negotiating his own contract*

"If God had an agent, the world wouldn't be built yet. It'd only be about Thursday."

> *Jerry Reynolds, Sacramento Kings player personnel director*

"You don't need a lawyer to tell the club you had a lousy year."

> Bill Stoneman, on not using an agent to renegotiate his contract

"What do you have when you've got an agent buried up to his neck in sand? Not enough sand."

> Pat Williams, general manager of the Orlando Magic

AIRPLANES

"This plane isn't going to crash. I'm on it."

> Muhammad Ali, speaking to a seat-mate on a rough flight

"They keep me pretty much in the dark about everything. If it had blown up, I wouldn't have known anything about it."

> Dennis (Oil Can) Boyd, hearing about a bomb threat on the plane he was flying on after it had arrived

"There won't be much of a delay. We only had to change a spark plug and 30 pairs of shorts."

> Don Drysdale, on the emergency landing of the Dodgers' private jet

"I don't think we could have won that game if we didn't have that plane."

> Dick Motta, on the importance of the Sacramento Kings having a private jet with a road record of 1 and 40 in 1990

"We've got a problem here. Luis Tiant wants to use the bathroom, and it says no foreign objects on the toilet."

> Graig Nettles, on an airline flight with his Cuban teammate

"All the time it's fasten your goddamn seat belt. But how come every time I read about one of those plane crashes, there's 180 people on board, and all 180 die? Didn't any of them have their seat belts fastened?"

> Fred Talbot, former major-league pitcher

"I like airline food."

> *Melvin Turpin, on claiming over the telephone that he weighed 265 pounds and then flying in the next day and weighing in at 282 pounds*

"First time all year he's circled the bases."

> *Dick Williams, on catcher John Tamargo's tumbling through the baggage chute at Doral Airport*

ALUMNI

"Cattle have no alumni."

> *Sammy Baugh, on why he retired to raise cattle*

"I'm not going to wear this for at least 24 hours. After 2–9 and 1–10 seasons, I'm a little edgy about anything that ticks."

> *Lee Corso, after receiving a watch as a gift from alumni*

"I always preferred a running offense, but I was smart enough to put in one long incomplete pass per quarter just for the alumni."

Duffy Daugherty, on his coaching philosophy

"I ask them to give us a lot of money, but not their two cents."

Joe Paterno, on alumni boosters

"A good season for the alumni is when the team goes 11–0 and the coach gets fired."

Pepper Rodgers

"My biggest problems are defensive linemen and offensive alumni."

Bo Schembechler

"We win, or the alumni bash in our teeth."

Jim Valvano, on the dental plan at North Carolina State

"I'm like a whale. Every once in a while I resurface."

> *Don Aase, on another pitching come-*
> *back*

"I didn't try too hard. I was afraid I'd get emotionally involved with the cow."

> *Rocky Bridges, on finishing second in*
> *a milking contest*

"When Larry Csonka goes on safari, the lions roll up the window."

> *Monte Clark*

"Joe Greene was on 'Wild Kingdom' once, and they shot him."

> *Don Rickles*

"I can't throw one, so I bought one."

> *Curt Schilling, major-league pitcher,*
> *on buying a dog and naming it Slider*

ARCHERY

"I don't know, I've never shot standing up."

> *Neroli Fairhill, Olympic archer from New Zealand, who was asked if his wheelchair was a hindrance*

"It's like, how long can you watch archery?"

> *Paul Wylie, Olympic silver medal winner, on the excitement of watching compulsory figures for ice skaters*

ARM WRESTLING

"You get guys from MIT and guys who can't spell MIT."

> *Sylvester Stallone, on the universal appeal of arm wrestling*

ARTIFICIAL TURF

"If a horse can't eat it, then I don't like it."
Dick Allen, on artificial turf

"I don't know. I never smoked AstroTurf."
Tug McGraw, on whether he favored grass or artificial turf

"It will revolutionize baseball. It will open a whole new area of alibis for the players."
Gabe Paul, on artificial turf

ATTENDANCE

"Very much so. I didn't have to work on visual signs for when the crowd gets noisy."
Bill Fitch, asked if small crowds had an effect on his coaching strategy

"It looked like a graveyard with lights."

Whitey Herzog, on a small crowd at Busch Stadium

"It was the first time in history that everyone in the stands got a foul ball."

Dave LaPoint, on 1,632 fans who showed up at Candlestick Park

"Some people have those games where you guess the number of people in the park. Here you have to identify them, too."

Lee Mazzilli, on a small crowd at Three Rivers Stadium

"At least now I can find my wife in the crowd."

Joe C. Meriweather, on declining attendance at Kansas City Kings games

"This would have been a good year to paint the seats."

Gerald Perry, Braves outfielder, on poor attendance in Atlanta

"Sometimes you walk out onto the field and wonder if they've opened the gates."

> *R. J. Reynolds, on low attendance at*
> *Three Rivers Stadium*

"I don't know if that was the attendance figure or the year Nolan Ryan was born."

> *Mike Scott, after an attendance figure*
> *of 1,938 was put on the scoreboard in*
> *Atlanta*

"The attendance was announced as 17,780, but 15,000 of them were disguised as empty seats."

> *George Vecsey, on claims by New York*
> *Titans announcer Harry Wisner that*
> *there were 17,780 in attendance at a*
> *Titans football game*

"Harry counts fingers instead of behinds."

> *Dick Young, on Harry Wisner, who*
> *frequently inflated attendance figures*

"I wish my name was Tom Kite."

Ian Baker-Finch, on signing a lot of autographs

"Sometimes I sign autographs; sometimes I don't. Personally, I think anyone who saves autographs is crazy."

Bob Gibson

"Any ballplayer that doesn't sign autographs for little kids ain't an American. He's a Communist."

Rogers Hornsby

"I didn't know whether to check him or ask for his autograph."

Bill Houlder, on his first shift in the NHL when he had to check Wayne Gretzky

" 'Sorry, Mickey,' the Lord said, 'but I wanted to give you the word personally. You can't go to heaven because of the way you acted down on earth, but would you mind signing a dozen baseballs?' "

Mickey Mantle, on a recurring nightmare

"It was fun until a kid came up to me and said, 'My dad says you're getting old, you're going to die, and your autograph will be valuable.' "

Warren Spahn, on an autograph show

"Once someone in Washington brought this picture up to me, and I wrote, 'Do good in school.' I looked up, this guy is 78 years old."

Casey Stengel

"I love signing autographs. I'll sign anything but veal cutlets. My ballpoint pen slips on veal cutlets."

Casey Stengel

"His affability quotient has improved greatly since he discovered he could make a living by being nice."

George Vecsey, on Mickey Mantle's making money by signing autographs at card shows

"Racing is 99 percent boredom and 1 percent terror."
Geoff Brabhan

"You win some, lose some, and wreck some."
Dale Earnhardt

"All I had to do is keep turning left."
George Robson, after winning the 1946 Indianapolis 500

AWARDS

"Being a champion is all well and good, but you can't eat a crown."
Althea Gibson, after retiring from tennis

"I will perish this trophy forever."
Johnny Logan, after receiving an award

BACKUPS

"It's kind of difficult to introduce a guy you hope gets the flu every week."

> *Gary Hogeboom, introducing Cowboys starting quarterback Danny White at a banquet*

"I've graduated from clipboard to headset."

> *Cliff Stoudt, on moving from the Steelers' number 3 to number 2 quarterback*

BAD TEAMS

"How many Nordiques does it take to change a tire? Only one, but they'll all be there if it's a blowout."

> *Anonymous, on a bad Quebec Nordiques team*

"We were tipping off our plays. Whenever we broke from the huddle, three backs were laughing and one was pale as a ghost."

John Breen, former general manager of the Houston Oilers, on a bad Oilers team

"Our 1976 White Sox team was so bad that by the fifth inning Bill Veeck was selling hot dogs to go."

Ken Brett

"I managed a team that was so bad, we considered a 2-and-0 count on the batter a rally."

Rich Donnelly, Pirates coach

"Well, at least it's a good way to break in equipment."

Grant Fuhr, on all the goals he has given up playing for the Toronto Maple Leafs

"It was unbelievable in Chicago. You felt you had to pitch a shutout to tie."

Rich Gossage, on the 1976 White Sox

"The fans like to see home runs, and we have assembled a pitching staff for their enjoyment."

> Clark Griffith, on a pitching-poor
> Washington Senators team

"Forget the pitcher; send the guy who hit the foul."

> Charlie Grimm, manager of a weak-
> hitting Cubs team, after hearing a
> report from a scout who saw a pitcher
> throw a perfect game, with the only
> ball hit out of the infield a foul fly

"We formed a booster club in Utah, but by the end of the season it had turned into a terrorist group."

> Frank Layden, on a bad Utah Jazz
> team

"You mean in the state."

> Abe Lemons, at the time the Univer-
> sity of Texas basketball coach, asked if
> his team should be ranked in the Top
> 20

"I always liked working Indians games because they were usually out of the pennant race by the end of April, and there was never too much pressure on the umpires."

> Ron Luciano, former major-league umpire

"Sure, we went 0–14 last year, but we'll be back . . . maybe not in this century, though."

> John McKay, former coach of the Tampa Bay Buccaneers, speaking in 1977

"I think it's a good idea."

> John McKay, on what he thought of the team's execution

"Coaching that team is like having a window on the seat of the *Hindenburg*."

> Bob Plager, on rumors about being named the coach of the Toronto Maple Leafs

"They got Magic, and we get tragic."

> Jerry Reynolds, Sacramento GM, on comparing the Lakers to the Kings

"They overwhelmed one opponent, underwhelmed 10, and whelmed one."

> *Red Smith, on the 1958 Green Bay Packers team that had a record of 1–10–1*

"We were so bad last year, the cheerleaders stayed home and phoned in their cheers."

> *Pat Williams, on a bad Orlando Magic team*

BASEBALL

"You spend a good piece of your life gripping a baseball, and it turns out it was the other way around all the time."

> *Jim Bouton*

"Haven't they suffered enough?"

> *Beano Cook, on giving free baseball passes to the former hostages in Iran*

"The first big-league game I ever saw was at the Polo Grounds. My father took me. I remember it so well—the green grass and green stands. It was like seeing Oz."

John Curtis, former major-league pitcher

"Baseball is the only sport I know that when you're on the offense the other team controls the ball."
Ken Harrelson

"Baseball is a lot like life. The line drives are caught; the squibbles go for base hits. It's an unfair game."
Rod Kanehl

"Baseball is the belly button of society. Straighten out baseball and you'll straighten out the rest of the world."
Bill Lee

"Baseball is a lot like the army—there aren't many individuals. About the only difference is that baseball players get to stay in nice hotels instead of barracks."
Bill Lee

"I'm glad I don't play anymore. I could never learn all those handshakes."

> Phil Rizzuto

"If God wanted football to be played in the spring, he would not have invented baseball."

> Sam Rutigliano, former Cleveland
> Browns coach, on the USFL

"Ninety feet between bases is perhaps as close as man has ever come to perfection."

> Red Smith

"I've had many years that I was not so successful as a ballplayer, as it was a game of skill."

> Casey Stengel

"Good pitching always stops good hitting and vice versa."

> Bob Veale

"Baseball is like church. Many attend, but few understand."

> Wes Westrum

"The hitter asks the owner to give him a big raise so he can go somewhere he's never been, and the owner says, 'You mean third base.'"

Henny Youngman

BASEBALL CARDS

"They've taken my playing record off and put my managerial record on."

Sparky Anderson, on why he likes his latest baseball cards

"I wanted to be a big-league ballplayer so I could see my picture on a bubble-gum card."

Al Ferrara

"I felt like my bubble-gum card collection had come to life."

James Garner, after speaking at a sports celebrity dinner

"I could no longer fit on my baseball card."

Kent Hrbek, on why he lost 15 pounds

"**M**y mother must have sent them my baby picture; that was the last time I weighed 175."

> *Charlie Kerfeld, on why he was listed as 5'11", 175 pounds on his baseball card when he was 6'6", 245 pounds*

"**W**e live in a collecting society. Some people collect automobiles or guns; others just collect unemployment."

> *Bill Lee, on why people collect baseball cards*

"**T**hey should eat the bubble gum, the cards, first base, the mound—things of that nature. But bad statistics can't be properly digested, so they should eat the cards of only the good players."

> *Doug Rader, on advice he gives to youngsters on baseball*

BASEBALL COACHES

"**T**he best qualification a coach can have is being the manager's drinking buddy."

> *Jim Bouton*

"Statistics are about as interesting as first-base coaches."

Jim Bouton

"All coaches religiously carry fungo bats in the spring to ward off suggestions that they are not working."

Jim Brosnan

"I'd become a first-base coach in the big leagues."

Paul McGuire, on where he'd hide if he ever held up a Brinks truck

BASKETBALL

"If the NBA was on channel 5 and a bunch of frogs making love were on channel 4, I'd watch the frogs, even if they were coming in fuzzy."

Bobby Knight

"The invention of basketball was not an accident. It was developed to meet a need. Those boys simply would not play Drop the Handkerchief."

Dr. James Naismith, the man credited with inventing basketball

"I liked the choreography, but I didn't care for the costumes."

> *Tommy Tune, 6'6" dancer who was asked why he never considered playing basketball*

"This is the second most exciting indoor sport, and the other one shouldn't have spectators."

> *Dick Vertleib, former GM of the Golden State Warriors*

BEDS

"I ain't gonna sleep standing up."

> *Yogi Berra, on Murphy beds*

BEER

"How do you know? It could have been Schlitz."

> *Earl Campbell, after a bottle of beer was thrown at him and a security guard said, "That was bush."*

"Cold."

> *Bruce Collie, 49ers offensive lineman,*
> *on his favorite kind of beer*

"When I played for Doug Rader, we weren't allowed to leave the clubhouse until all the beer was gone."

> *Tim Flannery, on the disciplinary tactics of Rader*

"When I was with the Sixers, I drank Michelob. In Houston, I was forced to switch to Coors and Miller. Now with the Bulls, I have to start all over with Budweiser."

> *Caldwell Jones, on adjusting to new teams after various trades*

"I really like your beer."

> *Dave LaPoint, after meeting then vice president Bush*

"If I were a Tibetan priest and ate everything perfect, maybe I'd live to be 105. The way I'm going now, I'll probably only make it to 102. I'll give away three years to beer."

> *Bill Lee*

"He's the kind of guy who would throw a beer party and then lock the bathroom door on you."

> *George Raveling, on Bobby Knight*

"I'm going to stop drinking 30 beers a day."

> *Craig Stadler, on how he is going to lose 35 pounds*

BENCH

"I've been sitting on the bench so long, the kids are beginning to call me Judge."

> *Gene Hermanski, longtime major leaguer*

"I told you we'd improve our bench."

> *Jack McKeon, on construction of new seats in the dugout at San Diego*

"The way he fielded ground balls, I knew he was going to wind up on the bench."

> *Sam Mele, on his teammate from college, Judge Burton Roberts*

"I occasionally get birthday cards from fans. But it's often the same message: they hope it's my last."

Al Foreman, former major-league umpire

"On Father's Day, we again wish you all happy birthday."

Ralph Kiner

"We were going to get a birthday cake, but we figured you'd drop it."

Casey Stengel, to legendary klutz Marv Throneberry

BODY PARTS

"Right now I feel that I've got my feet on the ground as far as my head is concerned."

Bo Belinsky

"If you took those two legs and barbecued them, you'd have enough to feed a family for a month."

> *Larry Bowa, on former teammate Greg Luzinski*

"Not unless they have Dutch elm disease."

> *Rob de Castella, marathoner, on being asked if it was a problem that his legs looked like tree trunks*

"The boy's got talent and desire, but he ain't got no neck."

> *John McGraw, on Hack Wilson*

"Damn, that's the same one I broke a couple of years ago."

> *Joe C. Meriweather, on breaking his nose*

"They wanted an arm and a leg."

> *Martina Navratilova, on why she never insured her left arm*

37

"They examined all my organs. Some of them are quite remarkable, and others are not so good. Several museums are bidding on them."

Casey Stengel

"Let them hit you. I'll get you a new neck."

Casey Stengel, offering advice to Elio Chacon

"They're so big they're able to Palm Sunday."

Peter Vecsey, on George McGinnis's hands

BOOKS

"How did yours come out?"

Yogi Berra, to Dr. Bobby Brown, reading Gray's Anatomy while Yogi was reading a comic book

"I read Billy Martin's autobiography, and when I woke up the next day I beat the hell out of my pillow."

Lefty Gomez

"Before he writes a book, he's got to read one."

Dallas Green, on Rickey Henderson threatening to write a tell-all book about the Yankees

"If all his old girlfriends buy it, it'll be a bestseller."

Hot Rod Hundley's ex-wife, on his autobiography

"One of them has me dead already."

Mark Koenig, member of the 1927 Yankees, on why he doesn't trust books written about the team

"I passed my time reading a book. It was called J.F.K.—The Man and the Airport."

Joe Magrane, on what he did to pass the time when he was injured

"You have to give Pete credit for what he's accomplished. He never went to college, and the only book he ever read was The Pete Rose Story."

Karolyn Rose, Pete Rose's ex-wife

"Maybe I couldn't read books, but I sure learned to listen to guys who did."

> *Eddie Shack, former hockey great, on being uneducated but becoming very wealthy*

"I couldn't put it down."

> *Pat Williams, on why* The Miracle of Helium *was his favorite book of the year*

"Charles once told me he would write his autobiography as soon as he could figure out who the main character would be."

> *Pat Williams, on Charles Barkley*

BOREDOM

"I don't give a rap about baseball anymore. It's just too dull."

> *Joe DiMaggio*

"Dave Goltz blends in with the furniture."
Joe Garagiola, on Goltz's personality

"Steve Garvey is the kind of guy who for laughs does impersonations of Tom Landry."
Jay Johnstone

"Having to listen to someone talk about themselves when I want to talk about me."
Tom Paciorek, defining boredom

"After the Dodgers won the World Series, Burt Hooten painted the town beige."
Vin Scully, on Hooten's personality

BOWL GAMES

"The Rose Bowl is the only bowl I've ever seen that I didn't have to clean."
Erma Bombeck

"You can bet that their float will reach the judge's stand by January 6."

> Bob Hope, on hearing that the U.S. Post Office would have a float in the Rose Bowl Parade on January 1

"In 1983 we got official Holiday Bowl watches. This year they told us that if we come back they'll fix our official Holiday Bowl watches."

> Glen Kozlowski, on why he was so excited about returning to the Holiday Bowl in 1984

BOWLING

"One of the advantages bowling has over golf is that you seldom lose a bowling ball."

> Don Carter

"He doesn't look like an athlete. He looks like a bowler."

> Rich Donnely, on stout Pirates catcher Mike LaValliere

"Interest your kids in bowling. Get them off the streets and into the alleys."

Don Rickles

"When I was a kid, I actually believed that wiping out the pin boy was the object of the game."

Charles Rosen

"There weren't many alleys that would let me come back. I have an overhand delivery."

John Wayne, on why he gave up bowling

"You don't take planes when you travel with 20 bowling balls."

Mark Williams, on why he travels by van on the Pro Bowlers Tour

BOXING

"Boxing is like jazz. The better it is, the less people appreciate it."

George Foreman

"I could only spar with my sister, and Dad said I couldn't hit her in the face, chest, or stomach. So all she did was belt me around."

Judy Johnson, on why he took up baseball instead of boxing

"We've all been blessed with God-given talents. Mine just happens to be beating people up."

Sugar Ray Leonard

"Boxing is the best and most individual lifestyle you can have in society without being a criminal."

Randy Neumann

"Boxing is a great sport and a dirty business."

Ken Norton

"Unless you've been in the ring when the noise is for you, there's no way you'll ever know what it's like."

Sugar Ray Robinson

"This is the only sport in the world where two guys get paid for doing something they'd be arrested for if they got drunk and did it for nothing."

Mark Robson, director of the movie **Champion**

"But I'm not fighting one bum a month. I'm fighting three or four."

> Buck (Tombstone) Smith, answering his critics charges that his record of 110–2 was inflated because he fought a bum a month

"I have the heart of a racehorse trapped inside the body of a jackass."

> Tracy Steele, boxer, who lost six of his nine pro fights

"Anyone who says he loves this business is a guy you have to look at very carefully. There's nothin' to love about being hit on the head."

> Mike Weaver

"I was 6'1" when I started fighting, but with all the uppercuts I'm up to 6'5"."

> Chuck Wepner

BUILDINGS

"They have either the biggest linemen I've ever seen or the smallest building I've ever seen."

Tony DeMeo, Iona football coach, on an opponent

CAPTAINS

"What is a captain supposed to do—go out on the field before the game and decide whether to kick or receive?"

Graig Nettles, on being named the Yankees' captain

CARS

"Well, he'll have to call up a blacksmith."

Yogi Berra, after Billy Martin left his keys in the car

46

"By the end of the season I feel like a used car."
> *Bob Brenly, longtime baseball catcher*

"My coordination was so bad I had to pull my car off the side of the road to blow the horn."
> *Ellis Clary, former major-league baseball player*

"I'd rather have a Mercedes, but I guess a Porsche makes a nice summer car."
> *Rickey Henderson, on receiving a Porsche for breaking Lou Brock's stolen-base record*

"It doesn't fit through the Wendy's drive-in."
> *Scott Hoch, golf pro, on why he was trying to sell the Mercedes-Benz he won at a golf tournament*

"I felt like I collided with a Mercedes-Benzinger."
> *Dennis Lamp, on bumping into teammate Todd Benzinger*

"Stanley Roberts's Florida license says, 'Photo continued on other side.'"

> *Pat Williams, on the former Orlando Magic's heavyset center*

CARTOONS

"I'm like Daffy Duck in the cartoons. I'm black, I've got big feet, and I'm always bitching."
Billy Sample

CELEBRITIES

"It's not very often you get to see the Lone Ranger and Toronto the same night."

> *Bobby Bragan, on a special appearance by Clayton Moore, who played the Lone Ranger, on the same night they were playing the Blue Jays*

"Nobody can be a success in two national pastimes."
>*Jimmy Cannon, on the breakup of Joe DiMaggio and Marilyn Monroe's marriage*

"It was better than rooming with Joe Page."
>*Joe DiMaggio, on whether his marriage to Marilyn Monroe was good for him*

"We've been trying to get Elvis. He's been dead long enough."
>*Ray Foreman, speculating on his brother George's next opponent in the ring*

"He hits the ball 130 yards, and his jewelry goes 150."
>*Bob Hope, on playing golf with Sammy Davis, Jr.*

"Before the game they told me I looked like Babe Ruth. Then, in my bat against Don Carmen, I looked like Dr. Ruth."
>*John Kruk, on his resemblance to Babe Ruth*

"Every once in a while even Sinatra has to clear his throat."

> Tony LaRussa, on Dave Stewart's going through a pitching slump

"Does Mike Tyson live near here?"

> Nelson Mandela, asked if he had any questions while walking through Manhattan

"We gave all the other guys gas money. We gave him covered wagon money."

> Doug Melvin, Orioles assistant GM, on 36-year-old minor leaguer Daniel Boone

"He's such a perfectionist that if he were married to Dolly Parton he'd expect her to cook."

> Don Meredith, on Tom Landry

"I have always admired his training methods and devotion, but I didn't have the guts to tell him his acting stinks."

> Bill Musselman, former NBA coach, on meeting Chuck Norris

"If they want somebody to play third base, they got me. If they want somebody to go to luncheons, they should have hired George Jessel."

> *Graig Nettles, on skipping a Yankees welcome-home luncheon in 1979*

"I guess I was the only NFL coach who was stupid enough to go along with it."

> *Bum Phillips, on appearing on a video with Boy George*

"Put it this way. If Richard Burton got sick the night before playing Macbeth in New York, he wouldn't be worried if Pee-wee Herman replaced him for a day."

> *Billy Ray Smith, on replacement players taking over for the regulars during the football strike*

"As a football player at Princeton, I always felt like Dolly Parton's shoulder straps—I knew I had a job to do, but I felt totally incapable of doing it."

> *Jimmy Stewart*

"Is that called 'dustin' Hoffman'?"

> *Joe Torre, on a brushback pitch thrown at Glenn Hoffman*

"It was like Arnold Schwarzenegger challenging Farrah Fawcett to a bench press in a Nautilus center."

> *Dick Vitale, on Syracuse playing Brown in the NCAA Tournament at the Carrier Dome, Syracuse's home stadium*

CHEAPSKATES

"Yeah, but in those days I was being paid by Branch Rickey."

> *Dizzy Dean, on weighing 240 pounds when his playing weight was 160 pounds*

"Of course, he's still got it."

> *Dave Marr, hearing that legendary cheapskate Sam Snead got only $500 for winning the British Open in 1946*

"Tommy Hearns squeezes a nickel so tight, the Indian sits on the buffalo."

> *Irving Rudd*

"If you could get the digging rights to Sam's backyard, you'd never have to work again in your life."

Doug Sanders, on Sam Snead

"Every year Tommy offers $50,000 to the family of the unknown soldier."

Don Sutton, on Tom Lasorda

CHEATING

"I used to play golf with a guy who cheated so badly that he once had a hole in one and wrote down zero on the scorecard."

Bob Bruce

"Who is this guy Queensberry? I don't see anything wrong in sticking your thumbs into any guy's eye. Just a little."

Tony Galento, mocking the marquis of Queensberry boxing rules

"Isn't it fun to go out on the course and lie in the sun?"

Bob Hope, on cheating in golf

"We just wanted to win enough to be investigated."

Dick Jackson, Iowa alumnus, on the surprising success of the Iowa football team

"You might as well praise a man for not robbing a bank."

Bobby Jones, on penalizing himself a stroke that cost him a championship

"I have a tip that can take five strokes off anyone's golf game: it's called an eraser."

Arnold Palmer

"Golf is a game in which the ball lies poorly and the players well."

Art Rosenblum

"Gaylord Perry handed me a tub of Vaseline. I thanked him, and I gave him a sheet of sandpaper."

Don Sutton, on the Christmas gifts he exchanged with Perry

"My three best punches were the choke hold, the rabbit punch, and the head butt."

Chuck Wepner

"I own a gun."

> *Charles Barkley, on why he loves New York City*

"I miss America. I miss crime and murder. I miss Philadelphia. There hasn't been a brutal stabbing or anything here the last 24 hours. I've missed it."

> *Charles Barkley, asked if he missed America during the Dream Team's stay in Barcelona in the '92 Olympics*

"Philadelphia is somewhat of a racist city. . . . Let's not kid ourselves. There are just as many black racists as there are white racists. . . . People never say I'm wrong. They just say I shouldn't say it."

> *Charles Barkley*

"If the rest of Washington ran as efficiently as this football team, there wouldn't be any deficit."

> *Jeff Bostic, on the Redskins*

"Now that I'm in Detroit I'd like to change my name from M. L. Carr to Abdul Automobile."

M. L. Carr

"I hate coming to New York. I hate the city. I hate the tournament, and I hate Flushing Meadows. They could drop an A-bomb on this place."

Kevin Curran, on the U.S. Open

"Brooklyn is all right, but if you're not with the Giants, you might as well be in Albany."

Bill Dahlen, on what it meant to play for the New York Giants

"The place was always cold, and I got the feeling that the fans would have enjoyed baseball more if it had been played with a hockey puck."

Andre Dawson, on Montreal

"I love to wake up to garbage trucks and gunshots."

Diane Dixon, quarter-miler, on her decision to train in her hometown, Brooklyn

"No armed guards in the parking lot."
> *Mike Flanagan, on the difference be-*
> *tween training in Dunedin, Florida,*
> *and Miami*

"I could never play in New York. The first time I ever came into a game there, I got in the bullpen car and they told me to lock the door."
> *Mike Flanagan*

"I always thought of Pittsburgh as a dirty city and a blue-collar town. And that's exactly what I think of their football team."
> *Jean Fugett*

"People in New York have black teeth, and their breath smells of beer. And the men are even worse."
> *Charlie Kerfeld*

"The first thing they do in Cleveland, if you have talent, is trade you for three guys who don't."
> *Jim Kern*

"In San Diego, I could go into a supermarket and never get recognized. When I go into a store in Washington, I get little old ladies critiquing my game, and it's not always good either."

Jim Lachey, on Redskin fans

"The weather up here for the Jets game is unusually balmy, just like me."

Paul Maguire, on the weather in Buffalo before the Bills played the Jets

"I come from New York, where if you fall down someone will pick you up by your wallet."

Al McGuire

"If a contest had 97 prizes, the 98th would be a trip to Green Bay."

John McKay

"Hate the city, hate the ballpark, hate the Mets. Other than that, it's great."

Tom Pagnozzi, on New York City

"The Indians who sold that island for $24 made a hell of a deal."

Allie Reynolds, on Manhattan

"In Cleveland, pennant fever usually ends up being just a 48-hour virus."

Frank Robinson

"I'd rather be in jail in Sacramento than be the mayor of Boston."

Bill Russell

"The best thing about playing in Cleveland is that you don't have to make road trips there."

Richie Scheinblum

"Philadelphia is the only city in the world where you can experience the thrill of victory and the agony of reading about it the next day."

Mike Schmidt

"They told me to watch out for sharks. I saw a lot of bodies, but no sharks."

Bob Shirley, on his first boat ride around New York

"The first day I got there, I put my suitcase down, looked up at the Sears Tower, and said, 'Chicago, I'm going to conquer you.' When I looked down, my suitcase was gone."

James (Quick) Tillis

"Crime is down in Miami. They ran out of victims."

Pat Williams

"When I approached the checkout counter of a Miami store, the clerk said, 'Cash, check, or stickup?'"

Pat Williams

CLINICS

"When I give a lecture, I look for the guy who's taking notes. That's who I want to schedule next year."

Abe Lemons, on basketball clinics

CLOSE

"The only time close counts is in horseshoes and dancing."

Fred Haney

CLOTHES

"I don't know, but I'm sure not going to find it in Butte."

Bonnie Blair, in Butte, Montana, on the outfit she would wear at the Sullivan awards that would compare with that of fellow nominee and flamboyant dresser Florence Griffith Joyner

"He's the only guy I know who does his clothes shopping at the San Diego Zoo. He puts five animals in the endangered species list with one outfit."

Bob Brenly, on the wardrobe of Kevin Mitchell

"Horseracing means loud clothes."

Mrs. Heywood Hale Broun

"With all those guys in suits and ties on the bench, the sideline was beginning to look like the men's shop at Macy's."

Dale Brown, on why he cut the size of his coaching staff

"It's great to see Pinky Lee's estate has finally been settled."

Bob Costas, on Wimp Sanderson's multicolored sport jackets

"Look, show me something for about $300 from a sheep that's fooled around a little."

Chuck Daly, clotheshorse, on rejecting a $1,300 virgin wool suit

"Cedrick does not wear clothes. He wears costumes."

Earl Edwards, on the unique outfits of Cedrick Hardman

"I wish he'd decide which I was so I'd know what to wear."

> John Feinstein, after Bobby Knight called him a pimp and a whore for writing A Season on the Brink

"The people who were sorriest were my tailor, my furrier, and my shoemaker."

> Walt Frazier, after he was traded from the Knicks

"I'm fat, and I sweat a lot and don't want to ruin all my clothes."

> Don Haskins, college basketball coach, on why he always wears the same clothes

"I have too much money invested in sweaters."

> Bob Hope, on why he will never give up golf

"A sport where the competitors are dressed as dinner mints."

> Jere Longman, Philadelphia Inquirer writer, on Olympic figure skating

"Coaching is like being a king—it prepares you for nothing."

Herb Brooks

"Sure I would. I'd miss him too."

Frank Broyles, Arkansas athletic director, asked if he would like football coach Ken Hatfield as much if Arkansas lost half its games

"We're going to have a good year if our coaching staff lives up to its potential."

Russ Francis

"All it means is that when they fire me as coach it won't be by unanimous vote."

Mike Fratello, on being named vice president as well as coach of the Atlanta Hawks

"I guess I must have rated between two and five."

> *Mike Fratello, on being fired after management called him one of the top five coaches in the NBA*

"If you're a pro coach, NFL stands for *Not for Long*."
> *Jerry Glanville*

"If we win a big game, I like my players to be strong enough to carry me off the field."

> *Lou Holtz, on the importance of physical strength in his players*

"My athletes are always willing to accept my advice as long as it doesn't conflict with their views."
> *Lou Holtz*

"Three out of four are guaranteed to go up the middle."

> *Jeff Hostetler, on Joe Paterno golf balls*

"When we come out of the tunnel, we make sure never to stand next to coach McKay, because the fans throw beer at him."

> *Curtis Jordan, on what he learned when he played for the Tampa Bay Buccaneers*

"I stood up and yelled at my wife all week."

> *Johnny Kerr, on how he prepared for coaching a basketball legends classic game*

"That's one way to look at it. The other is that I haven't had a promotion in 21 years."

> *Tom Landry, on coaching the Dallas Cowboys for 21 years*

"The coach who thinks his coaching is more important than his talent is an idiot."

> *Joe Lapchick*

"Coaches have to watch for what they don't want to see and to listen to what they don't want to hear."

> *John Madden*

"A team should be an extension of the coach's personality. My teams were arrogant and obnoxious."
                    Al McGuire

"When you're hired, you're fired. The date just hasn't been put in."
                    C. M. Newton

"He's what's known as a contact coach—all con and no tact."
                    Bob Reinhardt, Georgia State basketball coach, on Oklahoma coach Billy Tubbs

"When Xavier McDaniel plays against Orlando Woolridge, it's a coach's dream—X vs. O."
                    Mychal Thompson

"I don't like all those TV time-outs. I run out of things to say to my team."
                    Jim Valvano

"Larry Brown is like Liz Taylor. Just when you think it's over, someone new is ready to walk him down the aisle."
                    Donnie Walsh

"Some would say it is a means of endurance; some would say it was a measure of insanity. Depending on the day, I would agree with both."

> *Paul Webb, Old Dominion coach, on winning his 500th game*

COLLEGES

"The only way I can make five As is when I sign my name."

> *Alaa Abdelnaby, on his academic career at Duke*

"You beat those guys and you've beaten history, an institution. You're famous for life."

> *Marvin Barnes, on what it would be like to beat UCLA*

"To beat a bunch of yuppies in uniform feels good."

> *Charles Burnham, linebacker on San Jose State, after they beat Stanford in football*

"No, but they gave me one anyway."
> *Elden Campbell, asked if he earned a degree from Clemson*

"We didn't win many games, but we could fix every gym we played in."
> *Gordon Chiesa, former Manhattan College coach, whose 12 players included seven who had over a 3.0 GPA and four others who were engineering majors*

"Me."
> *Duffy Daugherty, asked whom he was happiest to see returning to Michigan State*

"We'd like our receivers to have both, but if they had both, they'd be at USC."
> *LaVell Edwards, Brigham Young coach, on what is more important for receivers—speed or quickness*

"How could it be mental? I don't have a college education."
> *Steve Farr, asked if his shoulder soreness was mental*

"I wound up with more complete games than credits."

Mike Flanagan, on his pitching days at the University of Massachusetts

"Fred has opened up amazingly. Last time I phoned him he said three words—'Send me money.'"

Walt Frazier, on how college had broadened his brother Fred

"I believe in higher education. You know, 6'8", 6'9", 6'10"."

David "Smokey" Gaines, basketball coach at San Diego State

"This job is better than I could get if I used my college degree, which, at this point, I can't remember what it was in."

Bob Golic, on a two-year, $1.5 million contract

"He and I got along just fine."

Jud Heathcote, on his old press conferences at Montana, before moving on to Michigan State

"I never graduated from Iowa, but I was only there for two terms—Truman's and Eisenhower's."

> Alex Karras

"When I picked the course for them, I didn't realize that the instructor graded on a curve and that there were 24 Indians in the class."

> Abe Lemons, on how two of his players failed basket weaving

"It's the only place that I ever got offered a job where they had a school song."

> Abe Lemons, on why he took the coaching job at the University of Texas

"Only Thomas Edison could invent a course Washburn could pass."

> Jim Murray, on Chris Washburn's being accepted to North Carolina State with an SAT score of 470

"I understand the TV show 'That's Incredible!' has been filming on the USC campus. They shot 12 football players attending class at the same time."

> *George Raveling, then Washington State basketball coach, now USC basketball coach*

"My players can wear their hair as long as they want and dress any way they want. That is, if they can afford to pay their own tuition, meals, and board."

> *Eddie Robinson, Grambling football coach*

"If I ask a kid how he did on the boards, and he says 12 a game, I know he's not coming to Harvard."

> *Peter Roby, Harvard basketball coach*

"But the real tragedy was that 15 hadn't been colored yet."

> *Steve Spurrier, Florida football coach, telling fans that a fire at Auburn's football dorm had destroyed 20 books*

"I thought about changing it to 'Ponder Those Canines,' but it didn't seem to be in the spirit."

Henry King Stanford, University of Georgia president, on yelling 'How 'Bout Them Dawgs' out of his car window to a passing stranger

"Monday through Friday they want you to be like Harvard. On Saturday they want you to play like Oklahoma."

Jim Valvano, on college administrators

"The University of Maryland football team members all made straight As. Their Bs are a little crooked."

Johnny Walker, disc jockey in Baltimore

"I'm glad it happened in front of the library. I've always emphasized scholarship."

Doug Weaver, former Kansas State University football coach, on being hung in effigy

"Stacey was a bit disturbed by the salary cap when he came here. They didn't have one at UNLV."

> *Bob Weiss, on the Atlanta Hawks signing former UNLV star Stacey Augmon*

"They had a big scandal at his school—three players were found in the library."

> *Pat Williams, on Jim Valvano and North Carolina State*

"When I told my wife that I believed UConn would win the Big East tournament, she wanted to know why a team from Alaska got into the Big East tournament."

> *Vic Ziegel, on the University of Connecticut*

COMMITTEES

"A committee is usually a group of uninformed, appointed by the unwilling to accomplish the unnecessary."

> *Syd Thrift*

COMPARISONS

"There were the inevitable comparisons from Day One. But they ended on Day Two."

> *Len Elmore, who attended Power Memorial High School after Kareem Abdul-Jabbar*

"Anything he wanted to do, anytime he wanted to do it."

> *Ferdie Pachecko, on what Muhammad Ali would have done had he fought Mike Tyson*

CONTRACTS

"Just give me 25 guys on the last year of their contracts; I'll win a pennant every year."

> *Sparky Anderson*

"The first time I realized it was a nightmare was when I heard their salary demands."

> *Terry Bradshaw, on a dream in which he had 22 all-time football greats on his team*

"When you have a one-year contract, you want to stretch that year out as long as you possibly can."

> *Chuck Cottier, on showing up six days early for spring training*

"I don't mind paying a player, but I don't want to pay for his funeral."

> *Pat Gillick, on the three-year contract demands of 39-year-old Rico Carty*

"I heard he was embarrassed by Atlanta's $4.5 million offer. I don't want to add to his embarrassment."

> *Tom Grieve, Texas Rangers general manager, on why he didn't offer Bob Horner a contract*

"All coaches are in the last year of their contract, only some of them don't know it."

> *Dan Henning*

"Your life or mine?"

> *Whitey Herzog, on being offered a lifetime contract by 80-year-old Cardinals owner Gussie Busch*

"When Bruce left, I told him, 'You've taken care of your children, your grandchildren, their grandchildren, and your whole family tree. If I get fired in July, you can adopt Mary Lou and me.' "

> *Whitey Herzog, on Bruce Sutter's multimillion-dollar contract*

"A lifetime contract for a coach means if you're ahead in the third quarter and moving the ball, they can't fire you."

> *Lou Holtz*

"Halas was famous for being associated with only one club all his life—the one he held over your head during salary talks."

> *Bobby Layne, on negotiating contracts with George Halas*

"They wanted to buy up my contract, but neither had change for $20."

> *Abe Lemons, on two disgruntled alumni who wanted to buy up his contract*

"They can't take it back because of one game."

> *Robert Parish, on shooting three of nine the day after signing a $3.5 million contract*

"He's a marvelous animal. He doesn't even ask to renegotiate."

> *Bum Phillips, after a two-year-old horse he owned won its first race*

"It isn't every manager who's offered a multihour contract."

> *Connie Ryan, on his short stint as the Texas Rangers manager*

"He signed me to a multiday contract."

> *Pat Williams, former Philadelphia 76ers' general manager, on his relationship with owner Harold Katz*

CONVENTIONS

"Start a rumor that you're looking for a road game."
Abe Lemons, on the quickest way to draw a crowd at a basketball coaches' convention

COOKING

"I can always catch a couple of hours of sleep in front of it—and it takes me only three minutes."
Sparky Anderson, on his microwave oven

"Even Betty Crocker burns a cake now and then."
Bill Caudill, relief pitcher, after an off game

"My wife hates to cook, so I've started cooking a little more. I'm a great microwaver."
Ken Green, pro golfer

"When I got home after practice one night, my young wife met me at the door crying, 'Darling, the dog ate the meat loaf I made for you.' I took her in my arms and said, 'Stop crying, honey, I'll buy you another dog.'"

Abe Lemons, on his early years in coaching

HOWARD COSELL

"Sometimes Howard makes me wish I was a dog and he was a fireplug."

Muhammad Ali

"If you split this guy open, demons and poison would spill all over the floor. He's one of the least attractive human beings I've ever been associated with."

Bob Costas

"In the next issue of *Cosmopolitan*, Howard Cosell will be the centerfold with his vital organ covered—his mouth."

Burt Reynolds

"Not while I'm alive."

Irving Rudd, on Cosell's statement that he was his own worst enemy

"In one year I traveled 450,000 miles by air. That's 18½ times around the world or once around Howard Cosell's head."

Jackie Stewart

"I have tried terribly to like Howard, and I have failed miserably."

Red Smith

COUNTRIES

"An hour after the game, you want to go out and play them again."

Rocky Bridges, on playing a Japanese team in an exhibition game

"Japanese fans are very positive. They clap for everything, including incomplete passes. I might want to coach there at the end of my career."

> Jack Elway, former Stanford football coach

"I mostly stayed around the house. But I did take a hunting trip to one of those Canadian proverbs."

> Jim Gantner, on how he spent his off-season

"Six feet from the moose's behind."

> Clark Gilles, asked where his hometown of Moosejaw, Saskatchewan, was located

"The only English words I saw were Sony and Mitsubishi."

> Bill Gullickson, on playing baseball in Japan

"It's a jungle out there."

> Peter Koech, Washington State runner from Kenya, asked about training conditions in his homeland

"Now I'll get to see the real Big Red Machine."

Bill Lee, on going to China after playing the Reds in the 1975 World Series

"Tell them to get a 6'10" father and a 6'4" mother and head to America as quickly as possible."

Luc Longley, giving advice to friends from his homeland, Australia

"There ought to be a clause in our contract allowing us to veto a country."

Steve Renko, after being traded to the Montreal Expos

"You figure there's eight trillion people in China; and if she was number 1 there, it says something."

Pam Shriver, after barely beating Hu Na in a tennis tournament

"If that young fella was running for office in Israel, they'd have a whole new government over there, and he'd boss it just like he bosses practically every game he pitches."

Casey Stengel, on Sandy Koufax

"He's committed to us, and we're committed to him. We probably all ought to be committed."

> *Gregg Lukenbill, Sacramento Kings part-owner, after offering a contract extension of two years to coach Jerry Reynolds, who had a record of 49 and 93*

"If he played for me, I wouldn't handle him with a strong arm; I'd handle him with a straitjacket like the rest of the nuts."

> *Billy Martin, on Bill Lee*

"What makes him unusual is that he thinks he's normal and everyone else is nuts."

> *Danny Ozark, on Jay Johnstone*

"I was crazy when Jay was still in the crib."

> *Jimmy Piersall, on Jay Johnstone's claim that he was the biggest nut in baseball*

CROQUET

"Croquet was really my kind of sport. That big wooden ball is just laid there begging to be hit. And there are no curveballs in croquet."

> *Marc Hill, former major-league catcher*

CURFEWS

"He couldn't fool us. We could hear his footprints."

> *Johnny Logan, on manager Chuck Dressen's doing bed checks on his players*

"I have only one training rule—don't get caught."
> *Frank McGuire*

"You usually wind up staying up all night until your best player comes in."

> *John McKay, on why he doesn't have bed checks*

"All pro athletes are bilingual. They speak English and profanity."

> Gordie Howe

"My coach, Dean Smith, and coach Knight are about the same except for language."

> *Michael Jordan, on his college days at North Carolina and playing for Bobby Knight in the Olympics*

"It may throw us off course but never off curse."

> *Kevin Loughery, on NBA rules restricting coaches to limited sideline areas*

"I cussed him out in Spanish, and he threw me out in English."

> *Lou Piniella, on being thrown out of a game by umpire Armando Rodriguez*

"I'll never forget one of his pep talks before a Lakers game. There were 72 bleeps in it, and it was Christmas Day."

>*Paul Westphal, on former Celtics coach Tommy Heinsohn*

DEATH

"The Good Lord might not want to take me, but He might be after the pilot."

>*Bobby Bowden, on his fear of small planes*

"Hockey was my life. This could be my death after life."

>*Gerry Cheevers, after getting off to a 3–9–1 start during his first year as a coach*

"I don't want to achieve immortality by making the Hall of Fame. I want to achieve immortality by not dying."

>*Leo Durocher*

"If Casey Stengel were alive today, he'd be spinning in his grave."

Ralph Kiner

"It was named after my arm."

Tim McCarver, on why Tim McCarver Memorial Stadium in Memphis is called "Memorial"

"Start counting—he will get up at nine."

Wilson Mizner, after the death of boxer Stanley Ketchel

"They can put on my tombstone, 'He'd-a lasted a lot longer if he hadn't played Pittsburgh six times in two years.' "

Bum Phillips

"If I drop dead tomorrow, at least I know I died in good health."

Bum Phillips, after passing a physical exam

"Well, that kind of puts a damper even on a Yankee win."

> *Phil Rizzuto, on news that the pope had died in August 1978*

"You can have money stacked to the ceiling, but the size of your funeral is still going to depend upon the weather."

> *Chuck Tanner*

"I feel like a guy in an open casket at his funeral; everyone walks by and mumbles what a great guy you were, but you stay dead."

> *Tom Trebelhorn, on the sympathy he received after being fired by the Brewers*

"I woke up one morning, and I was in kind of a fog. I saw all the flowers, but I couldn't hear any music. I thought my wife had bought me a real cheap funeral."

> *Bob Uecker, on all the flowers he received in the hospital after a heart attack*

"I just hope that when Gene Sullivan dies and goes to heaven, he doesn't find that the admitting is done by a selection committee."

> *Reverend E. Corbette Walsh, on Gene Sullivan, Loyola University (Chicago) coach, whose team didn't get into any postseason tournaments after winning 19 and 20 games in the previous two years*

DEFENSE IN BASEBALL

"He's not at his locker yet, but four guys over there are interviewing his glove."

> *Rex Barney, on Brooks Robinson*

"I hear it has an oversized glove compartment."

> *Johnny Bench, on Brooks Robinson's winning a car for being the 1970 World Series MVP*

"Is his first name Elmer? Because every time I look at the box score I see *E Concepcion*."

> *Larry Bowa, on the fielding of Dave Concepcion*

"I am not going to close my eyes this year when I go after pop-ups."

Paul Casanova

"I think, if I'm a bad outfielder, where does that put him?"

Jack Clark, on the fielding of George Foster

"He improved greatly in his ninth season. He still hadn't caught a ball, but he was getting a lot closer."

Gordon Cobbledon, on the legendary bad fielding of Babe Herman

"I've seen better hands on a clock."

Mel Durslag, after Dodgers shortstop Bill Russell had five errors in a doubleheader

"They want me to play third like Brooks Robinson, but I think I play it more like Mel Brooks."

Tim Flannery

"He was the only player in the majors who could lose a ground ball in the sun."

Joe Garagiola, on pitcher Billy Loes

"Has anybody ever satisfactorily explained why the bad hop is always the last one?"

Hank Greenwald

"He was a helluva hitter, but he had iron hands. You couldn't play him on rainy days; his hands would rust."

Ed Kranepool, on the fielding of Chuck Hiller

"It's not that Reggie is a bad outfielder. He just has trouble judging the ball and picking it up."

Billy Martin, on Reggie Jackson

"In the outfield, fly balls are my only weakness."

Carmelo Martinez

"I can't play perfect every day."

Teddy Martinez, after five errors in five games

"Every ball hit out there was a live cobra."

Gene Mauch, on the fielding of Brian Downing

"The only way to get the ball past him is to hit it eight feet over his head."

> *John McGraw, on Honus Wagner*

"Our fielders have to catch a lot of balls—or at least deflect them to someone who can."

> *Dan Quisenberry, on bad fielding by the Royals*

"He's the guts of the Angels, our triple threat. He can hit, run, and lob."

> *Merv Rettenmund, on Don Baylor's weak throwing arm*

"I've never seen anyone get hit by so many balls in the field without ever touching them as Enos Cabell."

> *Frank Robinson*

"He's the only defensive catcher in baseball who can't catch."

> *Casey Stengel, on catcher Chris Cannizzaro*

"Bobby Brown reminds me of a fellow who's been hitting for 12 years and fielding one."

Casey Stengel

"That ain't a third baseman. That's a fucking acrobat."

Casey Stengel, on Billy Cox

"Errors are part of my image."

Dick Stuart, former first baseman, nicknamed Dr. Strangeglove

"He wore a glove for only one reason. It was a league custom. The glove would last him a minimum of six years because it rarely made contact with the ball."

Frescoe Thompson, on Babe Herman

"Nick Etten's glove fields better with Nick Etten out of it."

Joe Trimble

"They had better defense at Pearl Harbor."

Andy Van Slyke, on the Pirates

"He plays like he's on a minitrampoline out there or wearing helium kangaroo shorts maybe."

Andy Van Slyke, on Ozzie Smith

DEFENSE IN FOOTBALL

"The good news is that our defense is giving up only one touchdown a game. The bad news is that our offense is doing the same."

Bobby Bowden

"Anytime your defense gives up more points than your basketball team, you're in trouble."

Lou Holtz, on his coaching days at the University of Minnesota

"They're so tough that when they finish sacking the quarterback they go after his family in the stands."

Tim Wrightman, on the Chicago Bears' defense

"It's really disgusting, isn't it, coming in here with a white uniform? It makes you feel like you're not playing a regular role. I'll probably get through the season with only two pairs of pants."

> *Brian Downing, on being a designated hitter*

"It's almost worth feeding him a couple of hits a game just to keep him in the outfield."

> *Billy Grabarkewitz, on how the DH rule would affect the play of Rico Carty, a good hitter but lousy fielder*

"I flush the toilet between innings to keep my wrists strong."

> *John Lowenstein, on being a DH*

DESSERT

"I'll have a pie à la mode with ice cream."

> *Johnny Logan*

"I lost five pounds and my driver's license."

> *Rocky Bridges, on his diet of two jiggers of Scotch and one jigger of Metrecal*

"Did you ever see a monkey with a cramp?"

> *Bill Lee, on his banana diet*

"After four days you're hallucinating, and after a week you want to go out and find a grapefruit farmer and blow his head off."

> *Frank Robinson, on a grapefruit diet*

"We've got Keeney on the lettuce diet. Unfortunately, he eats 40 pounds of lettuce a day."

> *Steve Sloan, on 6'6", 334-pound Texas Tech player Mike Keeney*

"We told Stanley to go on a water diet, and Lake Superior disappeared."

> *Pat Williams, on hefty center Stanley Roberts*

"It wasn't watching what I ate. It was watching what my friends ate."

Wilbur Young, Chargers lineman, on the toughest part of losing 85 pounds

DISCIPLINE

"If it was, Army and Navy would be playing for the national championship every year."

Bobby Bowden, asked if discipline was the key to winning

"When I discipline them, I make them play."

Abe Lemons, on hearing that Eddie Sutton disciplined a player by making him miss a game

DIVORCE

"My toughest fight was with my first wife."
Muhammad Ali

"My uncle always described an unforced error as his first marriage."

Bud Collins, tennis commentator

"Maybe I should get divorced every day. I'd be broke, but I'd also be in the Hall of Fame."

Keith Hernandez, on hitting two homers and seven ribbies on the night after his divorce became final

"My wife made me a millionaire—I used to have three million."

Bobby Hull, on his divorce

"Three of my wives were very good housekeepers. After we got divorced, they kept the house."

Willie Pep, boxing champion, on being divorced six times

"The next time I marry it'll be a man, and with my luck he'll get pregnant."

Joe Pepitone, on his many divorces

"He didn't play yesterday, and the manager got calls from his ex-wives to please put him in the lineup. They need the money."

Paul Popovich, on Joe Pepitone

"I only gave up three runs—Rosie gets half of every-thing."

Jose Rijo, on giving up six runs in an exhibition game while in the middle of a divorce

"It was a friendly divorce. She left me the piano and the lawn mover; I couldn't play either one."

Lee Trevino

DOCTORS

"When I was growing up I wanted to be a neurosur-geon, and even though some people think I haven't done much since I turned pro, I'd have to be a damn good surgeon to make what I'm making."

Kathy Horvath, pro tennis player

"Doctors bury their mistakes; we still have ours on scholarship."

> *Abe Lemons, on the difference between doctors and coaches*

"Finish last in your league and they call you Idiot. Finish last in medical school and they call you Doctor."

> *Abe Lemons, on the unfairness of being a coach*

"Remember, half the doctors in the country graduated in the bottom half of their class."

> *Al McGuire, on why athletes shouldn't be criticized for academic problems*

"He had such lousy hands when he played third, I wouldn't want him to operate on me."

> *Gene Woodling, on former teammate turned doctor, Bobby Brown*

DOUBLEHEADERS

"I never knew anybody who said they like doubleheaders except Ernie Banks, and I think he was lying."
Mike Hargrove

DRAFTS

"Whenever I look at the Jets' draft choices and see no guards among them, I consider that a real good draft."
Dave Herman, at the time a New York Jets guard

DRINKING

"Drinking is not a spectator sport."
Jim Brosnan

"I could use a triple double myself right now."

Skip Caray, Atlanta Hawks announcer, after Magic Johnson had a triple double against the Hawks

"Van Mungo likes to drink a bit. Anything. Even hair tonic."

Leo Durocher

"I can tell you Billy has a great heart, but I can't vouch for his liver."

Whitey Ford, on Billy Martin

"It depends on the length of the game."

King Kelly, when asked if he drinks during the games

"I must have. I remember the bar across the street."

Rod Laver, on whether he played a certain tournament in New Jersey

"He has a lot of things going for him. He's Irish Catholic, he laughs at my jokes, and his dad owns a bar."

Frank Layden, on John Stockton

"It's a lot easier when you're starting, because when you're starting you can pick your days to drink."

> *Bill Lee, on the advantages of starting over relieving*

"I had bad days on the field. But I didn't take them home with me. I left them in a bar along the way home."

> *Bob Lemon*

"Because of our great wines."

> *Michel Lourie, French track coach, on why France doesn't produce great athletes the way it produces great wine*

"There is much less drinking now than there was before 1927, because I quit drinking on May 24th, 1927."

> *Rabbit Maranville*

"If you drink, don't drive. Don't even putt."

> *Dean Martin, on drinking and golf*

"Dick Radatz just spilled his cocktail."
> *Gene Mauch, on a wheelbarrow full of ice falling on the steps of the Montreal Expos' dugout*

"No, the fast highball."
> *Gene Mauch, on being asked if Dick Allen's weakness was a high fastball*

"The only kind of spirit you see today in baseball is the kind you drink."
> *Johnny Mize*

"The first time I played the Masters I was so nervous I drank a bottle of rum before I teed off. I shot the happiest 83 of my life."
> *Chi Chi Rodriguez*

"No, thanks, I don't drink."
> *Jeff Stone, asked if he wanted a shrimp cocktail with dinner*

"The cops picked me up on a street at 3:00 A.M. and fined me $500 for being drunk and $100 for being with the Phillies."

Bob Uecker

"I see three baseballs, but I only swing at the middle one."

Paul Waner, on hitting well after a drinking spree

"The way he handled the pitcher was that you had to go drinking with him."

Bob Watson, on Astros pitching coach Jim Owens

DRUG TESTS

"They didn't mind after they found out they didn't have to study for it."

Mack Brown, former Tulane football coach, on how his players reacted to taking drug tests

"No way. I hate needles."

> *Bob Kearney, on whether he favored*
> *drug testing for major leaguers*

"Imagine the road to New Orleans starting in the bathroom."

> *Gary Leonard, Missouri center, on be-*
> *ing tested before the NCAA Tourna-*
> *ment began (the Final Four was*
> *played in New Orleans)*

"I'm in favor of it as long as it's multiple choice."

> *Kurt Rambis, on drug testing*

EGO

"When you're as great as I am, it's hard to be humble."

> *Muhammad Ali*

"I'll beat him so bad he'll need a shoehorn to put his hat on."

> *Muhammad Ali, on fighting Floyd*
> *Patterson*

107

"If this plane goes down, you won't even get in the small print."

> *Michael Cooper, former Los Angeles Laker, to the L.A. Raiders after finding out that they were on the same plane as the Lakers*

"The planes at LaGuardia had better not fly too low when I'm at bat."

> *George Foster, after being acquired by the New York Mets*

"You have to love talent, baby, and I have nothing but talent. Why, I amaze myself."

> *Ken Harrelson*

"I'm a legend. People aren't going to forget about me. I mean, when people forget about me, baseball is over. I rewrote the book."

> *Rickey Henderson*

"I'm still Reggie, but not so often."

> *Reggie Jackson, at age 38*

"You're only as good as your limitations, and I don't have any."

Edgar Jones, former Cleveland Cavaliers center

"He is unhappy everywhere except in his own arms."
Dave Kindred, on Eric Dickerson

"There isn't enough mustard in the world to cover Reggie Jackson."
Darold Knowles

"Nobody has to tell Richard Burton he was a great actor. Nobody has to tell Frank Sinatra he is a great singer. Nobody has to tell Robert Wagner he's handsome. Nobody has to tell me I'm a good manager."
Tommy Lasorda

"I'll always be number 1 to myself. The legend just won't be there. I guess I'll go home and watch my own videos."

Moses Malone, on not making the All-Star game for the first time in 12 years

"I think he'll eventually have the credentials to back up everything he thinks of himself."

Jack McCloskey, on Christian Laettner

"Someday he can tell his grandchildren he hit against me."

Doc Medich, on pitching to Hank Aaron

"I know you live in the country, but don't you have TV?"

Chris Mullin, after a fan was amazed when Mullin hit five shots in a row

"I can't wait until tomorrow. Why not? Cause I get better-looking every day."

Joe Namath

"Young man, you have the question backward."

Bill Russell, asked how he would have fared against Kareem Abdul-Jabbar

"Me. On instant replay."

Derek Sanderson, asked to name the greatest hockey player he ever saw

"Many times at the beach a good-looking lady will say to me, 'I want to touch you.' I always smile and say, 'I don't blame you.'"

Arnold Schwarzenegger

"It's hard to like a guy who wears the word Thrill on his helmet."

Dave Smith, on Will "the Thrill" Clark

"With my name, I will have to be either a flake or one of the game's greatest pitchers, and I'm not flaky."

Scipio Spinks

"That's pretty good considering that Dave's previous idol was himself."

Willie Stargell, on Dave Parker saying that Stargell was his idol

"Look, if Larry ever dreamed that he beat me, he'd apologize when he woke up."

Lee Trevino, asked if he were scared that Larry Ziegler was leading him in the first round of a tournament

"If I only had a little humility, I'd be perfect."
Ted Turner

ENTERTAINMENT

"Making movies is like playing baseball—the fun is the playing."
Robert Altman

"I can get to the bathroom on Monday morning without crawling."
Lyle Alzado, on how acting differs from playing football

"The singin's easy. Memorizin' the words is hard."
Rocky Graziano, on his singing debut

ENVIRONMENT

"You can't play on grass if there's no oxygen."
Pat Cash, on why he supports environmental causes

"We're a lot more comfortable breathing the air we can see."

> *Mychal Thompson, on why the Lakers play well in L.A.*

ERRORS

"Errors are a part of the game, but Abner Doubleday was a jerk for inventing them."
Billy Ripken

EUROPE

"You can't get up in the middle of the night and go get a Slurpee."

> *Tellis Frank, on the disadvantages of playing in Europe*

EXAGGERATION

"I never exaggerate; I just remember big."

Chi Chi Rodriguez

EXCUSES

"How can a guy win a game if you don't give him any runs?"

Bo Belinsky, after losing a game 15–0

"There are a thousand reasons for failure but not a single excuse."

Mike Reid

EXERCISE

"I watched aerobics on TV."

Rickey Henderson, on how he kept in shape during the off-season

"I can't afford to diet. It would wreck my image. I can't even afford to have a fat dog."
Jack LaLane

"I love exercise. I could watch it all day."
Bill Russell

EXPECTATIONS

"In the preseason someone said there's no way Michigan State can win the Big Ten title playing zone defense, playing a small center, and playing two freshmen in the starting lineup. Only trouble was that person was me."
Jud Heathcote, Michigan State coach,
after winning the Big Ten title

"Never win 20 games a year, because then they'll expect you to do it every year."
Billy Loes

"If we had one more center, we'd have one."
Jerry Reynolds, on his expectations
for the Sacramento Kings

"Dickey is teaching me all his experiences."

Yogi Berra, on learning about catching from Bill Dickey

"The problem is that when you get it, you're too damned old to do anything about it."

Jimmy Connors, on experience

"If experience was so important, we'd never have had anyone walk on the moon."

Doug Rader

EXPERTS

"An expert is an ordinary fella away from home."

Bum Phillips

"Football doesn't take me away from my family life. We've always watched films together."

Fred Akers, former University of Texas football coach

"I told them if our offense can produce as well as they can, we'll be a good football team."

Barry Alvarez, Wisconsin football coach, whose staff of assistant coaches had six babies during the off-season

"Today I told my little girl I was going to the ball-park; she asked, 'What for?' "

Dave Anderson

"It's a good thing Brian was a third child, or he would have been the only one."

Kathy Bosworth, on her son Brian

"The other night, my son was on his way to a party and I told him to have a good time. He snarled back at me, 'Don't tell me what to do.'"

Rocky Bridges

"When my father saw me play baseball, he got waivers from the rest of the family and traded me for a dog to be named later."

Jack Buck

"George probably figured that playing goal in the NHL was the quietest spot in his life. After all, he was the father of 22 children."

King Clancy, on hockey great Georges Vezina

"My daughter Kelly is a friend of Ken Boswell's daughter Ashley. They hadn't seen each other in a while, and Ashley asked my wife if Kelly had been traded."

Jerry DaVannon

"My father looked at the check and then told the scout, 'Throw in another hundred and you can take the rest of the family.'"

Joe Dugan, signed to a $500 contract in the early 1920s

118

"As in red light. You know, no more kids."

> *George Foreman, explaining why his*
> *fourth son and ninth child, George V,*
> *is nicknamed Red*

"They shouldn't throw at me. I'm the father of five or six kids."

> *Tito Fuentes*

"Bud Grant said he was quitting the Vikings in order to spend more time with his family. One hour later his wife accepted the job."

> *Jerry Girard*

"You'd better clap, or you're grounded."

> *Ken Griffey, Sr., on Ken Griffey, Jr.,*
> *clapping after his father hit a double*

"I think the only person who has liked our schedule so far is my son. He gets the car whenever I'm out."

> *Bob Hallberg, then coach at Chicago*
> *State, on having twice as many away*
> *games as home games*

"How can I retire when I have a daughter in college and a wife who's on the Top 10 in Shopping every year?"

Don James, on rumors about his retiring

"It's a one-two combination they're working on Tyson. His wife and his mother-in-law. That's a tough combination to beat."

Jackie Mason, on Mike Tyson's marriage to Robin Givens

"Sometimes I look on Roy as my nephew, but sometimes only as my sister's son."

Gene Mauch, on the inconsistent play of his nephew Roy Smalley

"What was the coach's record that year, Daddy?"

Daughter of Shelby Metcalf, after he read her "Cinderella" and they came to the part about the pumpkin turning into a coach

"I owe a lot to my parents, especially my mother and father."

Greg Norman

"We sometimes forget my daughter's age, but we know she's got 80,000 miles on her."

Frank Quillici, on his family's moving 12 times in 12 years

"Dad taught me everything I know, but he would never tell me anything he knew."

Al Unser, Jr., on his father

"Football has affected my entire family's lifestyle. My little boy can't go to bed unless we give him a two-minute warning."

Dick Vermeil

"I learned a long time ago to hire one with three kids. He'll be in the office working at eight every morning so he doesn't have to deal with getting the kids off to school."

Dick Versace, on how he hired assistant coaches

"I never heard my last name here. Every time the announcer would say 'Juan . . . ,' the fans would boo so loud I couldn't hear anything."

Juan Agosto, on White Sox fans

"Philadelphia fans would boo a funeral."

Bo Belinsky

"If the people don't want to come out to the park, nobody's going to stop them."

Yogi Berra

"Phillie fans would boo a wake."

Joe Dugan

"Eighty-five percent of the people in the country work, and the other 15 percent come out here and boo my players. It's a playground for them. Those fans are losers."

Lee Elia, on Cubs fans

"One thing you learn as a Cubs fan: when you buy your ticket, you can bank on seeing the bottom of the ninth."

> Joe Garagiola

"You would have thought that I was a Nazi in Jerusalem."

> Reggie Jackson, on how Orioles fans reacted to him

"Coaches who start listening to fans wind up sitting next to them."

> Johnny Kerr

"Most of them would heckle the Special Olympics."

> Dennis Lamp, on Blue Jays fans

"Who are you calling a fool? You paid to watch this game."

> Frank Layden, berating a fan who called a referee a fool during a miserable Utah Jazz game

"It was about three to one that I was not an SOB. But there were a lot of ones."

John McKay, on letters he got from fans as the Tampa Bay coach

"I've never had a crowd in the big leagues ever clap for me before. On opening day when I was with Boston, I got a standing boo."

Stan Papi, after getting three hits in a game

"Fans never fall asleep at our games because they're afraid they might get hit by a pass."

George Raveling

"Some of these people would boo the crack in the Liberty Bell."

Pete Rose, on Philadelphia fans

"First, you have to flunk an IQ test. Second, you have to be able to drink a gallon of beer. If you drink more than a gallon, they give you a seat in the front row behind the Boston bullpen."

Joe Sambito, on bleacher fans at Fenway Park

"Detroit fans don't know anything about baseball. They couldn't tell the difference between baseball players and Japanese aviators."
Mayo Smith

"Those Philadelphia fans are still amateurs in the booing department compared to those in Pittsburgh."
Dick Stuart

"Mention grace to the average White Sox player or fan and he thinks you're talking about a waitress he knows in a topless bar."
William Tammeus

"When there was an Easter egg hunt before a game in Connie Mack Stadium, there would be a few kids who wouldn't get any eggs. The crowd would boo them."
Bob Uecker

"The highlight of my career came in Philadelphia's Connie Mack Stadium, when I saw a fan fall out of the upper deck. When he got up and walked away, the crowd booed."
Bob Uecker

"My wildest dreams don't have basketball in them."

Bill Jones, coach of the Jacksonville University team, asked if a convincing victory had exceeded his wildest dreams

"When I was younger, yes."

Danny Murtaugh, asked on his 57th birthday if he could think of a better wish than winning the World Series

FANTASY CAMP

"He looks like a guy who went to fantasy camp and decided to stay."

Don Sutton, on heavyset John Kruk

"Lots of people look up to Billy Martin. That's because he just knocked them down."
Jim Bouton

"I thought I might become Rice-A-Roni."
Jim Colborn, after Jim Rice charged after him on the mound

"If a guy takes off his wristwatch before he fights, he means business."
Al McGuire

"The whole thing reminded me of the junior prom—not a lot of action; just a lot of guys standing around, watching what's going on."
Dan Quisenberry, on a baseball fight

"I'll take you and a player to be named later."
Dick Radatz, 6'6", 265 pounds, going after the 5'5", 165-pound Fred Patek during a bench-clearing brawl

"When we broke camp this spring, I fined Shirley for making the club."

> *Don Baylor, on flaky pitcher Bob Shirley*

"That's the first letter I got from Bill White where I didn't have to pay a fine."

> *John Kruk, on a letter from the National League president informing Kruk that he had made the All-Star team*

"Play him, fine him, and play him again."

> *Gene Mauch, on the best way to handle Dick Allen*

FISHING

"Man can learn a lot from fishing—when the fish are biting, no problem in the world is big enough to be remembered."

> *Oa Battista*

"Fishing, with me, has always been an excuse to drink in the daytime."
Jimmy Cannon

"There are only two occasions when Americans respect privacy, especially in presidents. Those are prayer and fishing."
Herbert Hoover

"Fishing seems to be the favorite form of loafing."
Ed Howe

"Fishing is a delusion entirely surrounded by liars in old clothes."
Don Marquis

"All you need to be a fisherman is patience and a worm."
Herb Shriner

"There ain't but one time to go fishin', and that's whenever you can."
Diron Talbert

"There is no use in walking five miles to fish when you can depend on being just as unsuccessful near home."

Mark Twain

FOOD

"Why does sour cream have an expiration date?"

Larry Andersen, pondering some of life's unanswerable questions

"Better make it four. I don't think I can eat eight."

Yogi Berra, on being asked if he wanted his pizza cut into four or eight slices

"No, the meat's too tough, and the horns get stuck in my teeth."

Yogi Berra, on being asked in Alaska if he wanted mousse for dessert

"OK, but no potatoes. I'm on a diet."

Yogi Berra, asked if he wanted french fries

"I prefer fast foods."

> *Rocky Bridges, on why he doesn't eat snails*

"The U.S. Open is the only place in America where you can't trade in your Mercedes-Benz for a hamburger."

> *Bud Collins, on the high prices at concessions at the Open*

"I no longer sleep. I roost."

> *Lee Corso, on all the chicken dinners he has been to*

"I should have known I was in trouble when I looked in the kitchen and they didn't have any Chinese cooking."

> *Sleepy Floyd, on getting a stomach virus after eating at a Chinese restaurant*

"He's got a nutritionist, and I've got room service."

> *George Foreman, on the difference in training styles between himself and Evander Holyfield*

"I told them sandwiches."

> *George Foreman, asked before an appearance on the TV show "Home Improvement" what he liked to build*

"The attendant asked, 'Is that for here or to go?' "

> *Jim Greenidge, 320-pound PR director of the Patriots, who ordered two large family buckets from Kentucky Fried Chicken*

"If you cut that big slob in half, most of the concessions at Yankee Stadium would come pouring out."

> *Waite Hoyt, on Babe Ruth*

"Saltwater taffy."

> *Caldwell Jones, on his favorite seafood*

"Thank God! They electrocuted the chef."

> *Abe Lemons, after the lights momentarily went out during a banquet*

"It's raining cats and appetizers."

> *Mike Littwin, Baltimore sportswriter, on a rainy day in Seoul, where it is a common practice to eat dog meat*

"I used to be to vegetables what Orson Welles was to pole vaulting."

> *Rick Majerus, the formerly heavyset Utah basketball coach who lost over 100 pounds*

"After the game, there'll be more food for everyone."

> *Tippy Martinez, on his reaction after 300-pound Tim Stoddard was traded*

"The last time-out was to take the sandwich order."

> *Ed Murphy, basketball coach at Mississippi, asked why he took a time-out with two minutes left, losing by 20 points*

"After all these years, it's still embarrassing for me to play on the American golf tour. Like the time I asked my caddie for a sand wedge and he came back ten minutes later with a ham on rye."

> *Chi Chi Rodriguez, on his Spanish accent*

"Tommy Lasorda will eat anything as long as you pay for it."

> *Joe Torre, on the formerly heavy Dodgers manager*

"One of the nice things about the Senior Tour is that we can take a cart and cooler. If your game is not going well, you can always have a picnic."
Lee Trevino

FOOTBALL

"If a man watches three football games in a row, he should be declared legally dead."
Erma Bombeck

"Baseball players are smarter than football players. How often do you see a baseball team penalized for too many men on the field?"
Jim Bouton

"The NFL, like life, is full of idiots."
Randy Cross

"Football isn't a contact sport; it's a collision sport. Dancing is a contact sport."
Duffy Daugherty

"It would have been worse if we hadn't blocked the kick after Toronto's second touchdown."

> *Alex Delvecchio, after the Red Wings lost to the Maple Leafs 13–0 in an NHL game*

"I'd catch a punt naked in the snow in Buffalo for a chance to play in the NFL."

> *Steve Hendrickson, former University of California player*

"Most football players are temperamental. That's 90 percent temper and 10 percent mental."

> *Doug Plank, Bears safety*

"The football season is like pain. You forget how terrible it is until it seizes you again."

> *Sally Quinn*

"Football features two of the worst aspects of American life—violence and committee meetings."

> *George Will*

"He sends them through a car wash."

> *Lynn Shackleford, on Bob Lanier's*
> *size-20 basketball sneakers*

"Dad, did they name the shoe after you, or were you named after the shoe?"

> *Trevor Smith, nine-year-old son of*
> *Stan Smith, on Smith's own line of*
> *Adidas footwear*

"Back home, the only thing we had with a pump was the well."

> *Dave Tippett, Washington Capitals*
> *winger, from Moosomin, Saskatche-*
> *wan, on sneakers with pumps*

"When you have a size-14 shoe, you land on your feet most of the time."

> *Sam Wyche, on being fired as the*
> *Bengals' head coach and getting the*
> *Tampa Bay job*

THE FUTURE

"If I could look into the future, I wouldn't be sitting here talking to you doorknobs. I'd be out investing in the stock market."

Kevin McHale, on the Celtics' prospects in an upcoming season

GAMBLING

"Any new system is worth trying when your luck is bad."

Heywood Hale Broun

"The urge to gamble is so universal and its practice so pleasurable that I assume it must be evil."

Heywood Hale Broun

"No wife can endure a gambling husband unless he is a steady winner."

Lord Dewar

"A man's gotta make at least one bet a day, else he could be walking around lucky and never know it."

> Jimmie Jones, former horseracing trainer

"Never bet on a dead horse or a live woman. Never play cards with a man with dark glasses or his own deck."

> Jim Murray

"I wouldn't bet on it. Whoops, wrong statement around here."

> Paul O'Neill, asked while Pete Rose was still managing the Reds if after going four for four on opening day, O'Neill would hit 1,000 for the season

"Munson hasn't done anything wrong. I'd bet my house on it."

> Joe Schmidt, after quarterback Bill Munson was asked to testify in a gambling inquiry

"Pressure is playing for $10 when you don't have a dime in your pocket."

> Lee Trevino

GAS

"It puzzles me how they know what corners are good for filling stations. Just how did these fellows know there was gas and oil under there?"
Dizzy Dean

"Since the fuel shortage, we Texans are wearing two-gallon hats."
Bobby Layne

"Gas costs $2.40 a gallon."
Frank Shorter, on why Finland has great distance runners

GIRLFRIENDS

"Being a decathlete is like having 10 girlfriends. You have to love them all, and you can't afford losing one."
Daley Thompson

"It took me 17 years to get 3,000 hits. I did it in one afternoon on the golf course."

Hank Aaron

"If you break 100, watch your golf. If you break 80, watch your business."

Joey Adams

"If it weren't for golf, I'd probably be a caddie today."

George Archer

"Golf is an awkward set of bodily contortions designed to produce a graceful result."

Tommy Armour

"Sometimes when I look down at that little white golf ball, I just wish it was moving."

Dusty Baker

"His driving is unbelievable. I don't go that far on my holidays."

Ian Baker-Finch, on John Daly

"Man blames fate for other accidents but feels personally responsible for a hole in one."
Martha Beckman

"I was three over: one over a house, one over a patio, and one over a swimming pool."
George Brett

"Golf is a game whose aim is to hit a very small ball into an even smaller hole, with weapons singularly ill designed for that purpose."
Winston Churchill

"I enjoy the *oohs* and the *aahs* from the gallery when I hit my drives. But I'm getting pretty tired of the *awws* and *uhhs* when I miss the putt."
John Daly

"Golf and sex are about the only things you can enjoy without being good at it."
Jimmy Demaret

"If there is any larceny in a man, golf will bring it out."
Paul Gallico

"The safest place would be in the fairway."

Joe Garagiola, on the best place for spectators to stand during celebrity golf tournaments

"In baseball you hit your home run over the right-field fence, the left-field fence, the center-field fence. Nobody cares. In golf everything has got to be right over second base."

Ken Harrelson

"If you watch a game, it's fun. If you play it, it's recreation. If you work at it, it's golf."

Bob Hope

"I've done as much for golf as Truman Capote has for sumo wrestling."

Bob Hope

"I'll take a two-shot penalty, but I'll be damned if I'm going to play the ball where it lies."

Elaine Johnson, after her tee shot hit a tree and caromed into her bra

142

"My best score ever is 103. But I've only been playing 15 years."

Alex Karras

"Find a man with both feet firmly on the ground and you've found a man about to make a difficult putt."

Fletcher Knebel

"If you think it's hard to meet new people, try picking up the wrong golf ball."

Jack Lemmon

"Coaches who shoot par in the summer are the guys I want on my schedule in the winter."

Abe Lemons, college basketball coach

"The rest of the field."

Roger Maltbie, asked what he had to shoot to win a tournament

"I played so bad I got a get-well card from the IRS."

Johnny Miller, on a terrible 1977 season

"Anything I want it to be. For instance, the hole right here is a par 47, and yesterday I birdied the sucker."

Willie Nelson, on what was par on a course he bought in Texas

"I'm playing like Tarzan and scoring like Jane."

Chi Chi Rodriguez

"Golf is the most fun you can have without taking your clothes off."

Chi Chi Rodriguez

"If I could have putted like this years ago, I'd own a jet instead of a Toyota."

Chi Chi Rodriguez, on his play on the Senior Tour

"If I'm going to miss putting, I want to look good doing it."

Chi Chi Rodriguez, on why he is reluctant to use a long-handled putter

"There are two things not long for this world—dogs that chase cars and pro golfers who chip for pars."

Lee Trevino

"The only problem is that it's hell to find your way home every night."

Lee Trevino, on playing on four different golf courses in the Bob Hope tournament

"Hold up a 1-iron and walk. Even God can't hit a 1-iron."

Lee Trevino, on how to avoid being hit by lightning

"I'm not saying my golf game went bad, but if I grew tomatoes they'd come up sliced."

Lee Trevino

"I tell myself that Jack Nicklaus probably has a lousy curveball."

Bob Walk, major-league pitcher, on how he handles frustrations as a golfer

"Let the teachers learn the kids English. Ol' Diz will learn the kids baseball."

Dizzy Dean

"I appreciate the support. But I can't believe they ended a sentence with a preposition."

Walter Palmer, pro basketball player, on fans displaying a sign that said 'Put Walter In'

GRAVE DIGGERS

"I'm good at it. In ten years no one's ever dug himself out of one of my graves yet."

Richie Hebner, on being a grave digger in the off-season

"I've buried people in better shape than I'm in."

Richie Hebner, after a two-mile run in spring training

"Always remember, morticians are the last people to let you down."

> Digger Phelps, on working for his father, who was a mortician

"I was able to send my girlfriends flowers every day."

> Digger Phelps, on being a mortician's son

GREATNESS IN BASEBALL

"Damn, I've got to face Dwight."

> Hubie Brooks, on being traded from New York to Montreal and being forced to hit against Dwight Gooden

"There was always Joe DiMaggio. If we had him, we could have won. But the Yankees had him, and he murdered everybody, including us."

> Joe Cronin, Red Sox Hall of Famer, on Joe DiMaggio

"If Satch and I were pitching on the same team, we'd cinch the pennant by July 4 and go fishing until World Series time."

Dizzy Dean, on Satchel Paige

"Without Ernie Banks, the Cubs would finish in Albuquerque."

Jimmy Dykes

"You used to think if the score was 5–0 he'd hit a five-run homer."

Reggie Jackson, on Willie Mays

"Blind people came to the park just to listen to him pitch."

Reggie Jackson, on Tom Seaver

"If he were playing in New York, there'd be a 5′ 8″ statue of him in Times Square."

Andy MacPhail, on Kirby Puckett

"Cobb lived off the field as though he wished to live forever. He lived on the field as though it was his last day."

Branch Rickey, on Ty Cobb

"The day Mickey Mantle bunted when the wind was blowing out in Crosley Field."

Robin Roberts, on his greatest All-Star game thrill

"He's baseball's exorcist—he scares the devil out of you."

Dick Sharon, on Nolan Ryan

"Throwing a fastball by Henry Aaron is like trying to sneak the sun past a rooster."

Curt Simmons

"When Sandy Koufax retired."

Willie Stargell, on his greatest thrill in baseball

"He's so good, I even worry about him in winter."

Ted Williams, on Bob Lemon

"We have 44 defenses for him, but he has 45 ways to score."

Al Attles, on Nate "Tiny" Archibald

"Michael is head and shoulders above us all. But Magic Johnson is the best player I've ever seen."

Larry Bird

"What's the matter with those guys? Don't they have cable up there?"

Antoine Carr, on the Chicago Bulls, who kept challenging David Robinson even though he blocked eight shots against them

"The thing about him is that you know he is going to get to the basket; you just never know how."

Bobby Jones, on Julius Erving

"I'd get real close to him and breathe on his goggles."

Johnny Kerr, on the best way to guard Kareem Abdul-Jabbar

"I'll always remember this as the night that Michael Jordan and I combined to score 70 points."

>*Stacey King, who had one point to Jordan's 69*

"I can't get my eyes off him. I think I'm in love."

>*Don Nelson, on Shaquille O'Neal*

"Magic is the best player who plays on the ground, and Michael is the best player who plays in the air."

>*John Paxson, on Michael Jordan*

"In my prime I could have handled Michael Jordan. Of course, he would be only 12 years old."

>*Jerry Sloan*

"You don't hesitate with Michael, or you'll end up on some poster in a gift shop someplace."

>*Felton Spencer, on Michael Jordan*

"It'll be like Halloween without Elvira."

>*Mychal Thompson, on Kareem Abdul-Jabbar's retiring from the NBA*

"Any living legend can take over a game in the last few minutes. Only Bird can take it over in the first few minutes."

Peter Vecsey, on Larry Bird

GREATNESS IN BOXING

"When God rang the bell and ended the fight, the world cried out for one more round."

Jesse Jackson, on Sugar Ray Robinson

GREATNESS IN FOOTBALL

"He's like a little sports car. He can stop on a dime and go zero to 60 in seconds."

Trace Armstrong, on Barry Sanders

"It's like standing blindfolded in the middle of Interstate 75, dodging the cars and trying to tackle the biggest truck out there."

Gary Burley, on Earl Campbell

"Every time I tackle Jim Brown, I hear a dice game going on inside my mouth."
Don Burroughs

"You go for something you think is there, and all of a sudden you don't have anything."
Edgar Chandler, on O. J. Simpson

"When you hit him at the ankles, it was like getting an electric shock. If you hit him above the ankles, you were likely to get killed."
Red Grange, on Bronko Nagurski

"Franco Harris faked me out so bad one time that I got a 15-yard penalty for grabbing my own face mask."
D. D. Lewis

"John Elway is an immediate cure for coach's 'burnout.' "
John Madden

"You came out hurting all over, and what didn't hurt didn't work."
Jim Otto, on facing Mean Joe Greene

"Shoot him before he leaves the dressing room."

Steve Owen, on the best way to stop Bronko Nagurski

"If he can't do it, then he sure knows where the stumps are buried."

Ara Parseghian, asked if Bear Bryant could walk on water

"Earl may not be in a class by himself, but whatever class he's in, it doesn't take long to call the roll."

Bum Phillips, on Earl Campbell

"Three or four men and a horse rolled into one."

Damon Runyon, describing Red Grange

"He was like Moby Dick in a goldfish bowl."

Steve Sabol, describing the greatness of Dick Butkus

"He's a cocky sumbitch. That's what makes him such a great player."

Phil Simms, on Lawrence Taylor

"If a nuclear bomb ever dropped on this country, the only things I'm certain will survive are AstroTurf and Don Shula."

Bubba Smith

"We hitched our wagon to a Starr."

Jim Taylor, explaining the greatness
of the Packers and their quarterback,
Bart Starr

"You've heard of people who zig or zag. Well, Elroy also had a zog and a couple of zugs."

Norm Van Brocklin, on Elroy "Crazy
Legs" Hirsch

GREATNESS IN GOLF

"Arnold Palmer is the biggest crowd pleaser since the invention of the portable sanitary facility."

Bob Hope

"When Jack Nicklaus plays well, he wins. When he plays badly, he finishes second. When he plays terrible, he finishes third."

Johnny Miller

GREATNESS IN HOCKEY

"What he does best is make you look bad."

Richard Brodeur, on Wayne Gretzky

"To get as many goals this year as Wayne Gretzky got last week."

Don Maloney, on his New Year's resolution

"What I want for Christmas is a Mike Bossy doll. Wind it up and he scores 60 goals."

Tom McVie

"I've said it before and I'll say it again: You're looking at the next scoring leader in the league when Wayne Gretzky decides not to be."

Warren Young, on Mario Lemieux

GREATNESS IN HORSERACING

"I could cut through the infield and she'd still beat me."

> *Braulio Baeza, on his horse losing by a wide margin to the legendary Ruffian*

"If I were young, fast, healthy, and had a lot of money and my whole sex life ahead of me, I'd retire—like Secretariat."

> *Dick Butkus*

"He was not a horse—he was Secretariat."

> *Bennett Liebman, New York State Racing Commissioner, on the death of Secretariat*

GREATNESS IN TENNIS

"She's like the old Green Bay Packers. You know exactly what she's going to do, but there isn't a thing you can do about it."

> *Arthur Ashe, on Martina Navratilova*

GREED

"I think greed is a terrible thing—unless you're in on the ground floor."

Yogi Berra

GROSS BEHAVIOR

"Boozer used to go into the clubhouse and spit on the ceiling. When it dropped back down, he would catch it in his mouth. He would try to turn guys' stomachs."

Clay Dalrymple, on the talents of teammate John Boozer

"When Leo touched his nose, it meant the hit-and-run was on. But there was one problem. The son of a gun was always picking his nose."

Herman Franks, on Leo Durocher

"He'll probably get 40 years—one for failing to report his income tax and the other 39 for his haircut."

Buddy Baron, on Pete Rose

"Now you look like a ballplayer. You're not so feminine looking."

Al Dark, forcing Ken Harrelson to get a haircut

"Hearing the crowd was great. It made what little hair I had stand on end."

Alex English, on a standing ovation after scoring 54 points in a game

"I don't have any more hair on my head than I need."

Joe Garagiola

"My decision to make goalkeeping a career might have something to do with it."

Eddie Giacomin, on having gray hair since the age of 19

"Anybody who has plastic hair is bound to have problems."

> *Jay Johnstone, on Steve Garvey*

"He spends more on a haircut than I do on a sport jacket."

> *Frank Layden, comparing his sartorial style with that of Pat Riley*

"It's not the legs that go first—it's the hair."

> *Pat Leahy, former 40-year-old place-kicker for the New York Jets*

"My arm could go every second day, but my hair needed four days rest."

> *Bill Lee, on pitching on a five-man rotation*

"With Michael, you just hope and pray a lot. You go to church and you try to talk about things Michael doesn't like to talk about—like baldness."

> *John Salley, on defending Michael Jordan*

"He really ought to dye his hair. It's embarrassing to find yourself tangling with a gray-haired man."

> *Jim Schoenfeld, on fighting with 39-year-old Henri Richard*

"I call it the 'Watergate.' I cover up everything I can."

> *Joe Torre, on his hairstyle*

"I had four maiden aunts who had hair just like it."

> *Donnie Walsh, Pacers' president, on not being bothered by the silver-white Caesar-cut hairstyle of former coach Dick Versace*

HALFTIME

"I left at halftime."

> *Andre Agassi, on what he thought of the play* Les Misérables

"Baryshnikov was booked. So we went with Barry."

> *Stan Kasten, Hawks' GM, on booking Dancing Barry for a halftime show in Atlanta*

"I give the same halftime speech over and over. It works best when my players are better than the other coach's players."

Chuck Mills

"If that guy makes a turnover, we're gonna be in deep trouble."

Rick Sund, on a halftime show at a Dallas Mavericks' game that featured a guy juggling chainsaws

HALL OF FAME — BASEBALL

"There was never any question about his courage. He proved it by getting married four times."

Jack Brickhouse, on being asked if Enos Slaughter was qualified for the Hall of Fame

"Now I guess I'm 'mongst them mortals."

Dizzy Dean, on his induction to the Hall of Fame

"The Hall of Fame is for baseball people. Heaven is for good people."

Jim Dwyer, on why Pete Rose should be in the Hall of Fame

"The Hall of Fame ceremonies are on the 31st and 32nd of July."

Ralph Kiner

"I'm always going to have trouble saying Mays, Musial, and Morgan in the same breath."

Joe Morgan, after being inducted into the Hall of Fame

"When I asked the baseball writers why they haven't elected me to the Hall of Fame, they told me they still thought I was playing."

Bob Uecker

"How did I feel when I heard the names? About the same way, I guess, that Columbus felt when he looked out from his ship and first saw land."

Dazzy Vance, on getting elected to the Hall of Fame

HALL OF FAME—
FOOTBALL

"Politics is an astonishing profession. It has enabled me to go from being an obscure member of the junior varsity at Harvard to being an honorary member of the Football Hall of Fame."

John Fitzgerald Kennedy

"A hotel operator called and said I had been indicted. I panicked and said, 'For what?'"

John Mackey, how he found out about being inducted into the Football Hall of Fame

HALL OF FAME—GOLF

"It was a great honor to be inducted into the Hall of Fame. I didn't know they had a caddie division."

Bob Hope, on his induction into the Golf Hall of Fame

HALL OF FAME—
SHUFFLEBOARD

═══════════════════════════════

"Let's be honest. Everybody wants to get in."

> Herbert Burns, curator of the Shuffle-
> board Hall of Fame, on why there is a
> screening process for induction into
> the Shuffleboard Hall of Fame

HEART

═══════════════════════════════

"My cholesterol level went down 30 percent while I was recruiting him."

> Kevin Bannon, coach at Trenton
> State, on recruiting Greg Grant, who
> worked in a seafood restaurant

"First triple I ever had."

> Lefty Gomez, on his triple-bypass
> surgery

"For a while I was eating so many oats, I started counting with my foot."

> *Rick Majerus, on dieting after heart surgery*

"When Charlie Finley had his heart operation, it took eight hours—seven just to find his heart."

> *Steve McCatty*

"Bobby Knight is a good friend of mine. But if I ever need a heart transplant I want his. It's never been used."

> *George Raveling*

"Wait a minute. I gotta consult my rabbi first."

> *Irving Rudd, on finding out his aorta would be replaced by a pig's bladder*

"It's like having heart attacks. You can survive them, but there's always scar tissue."

> *Sam Rutigliano, former Cleveland Browns' coach, on several last-minute defeats in 1978*

HEIGHT

"Fred Patek was so small when he was born that his father passed out cigar butts."

Joey Adams, on 5'5" former major leaguer Fred Patek

"I'm supposed to stop the puck, not beat it up."

Don Beaupre, on being a 5'7" goalie

"I can't miss a class. The professor doesn't have to call the roll to know I'm not there."

Tom Burleson, on being 7'4"

"He's the only coach in the NBA who can sleep in a pillowcase."

Skip Caray, on the diminutive Cotton Fitzsimmons

"It's good to have a lineman you can look straight in the belly button."

Larry Csonka, on the 6'6", 285-pound Gordon King

"He's so tall that if he fell down, he'd be halfway home."

Darryl Dawkins, on 7'6" Manute Bol

"We had to go to Toys R Us."

Bob Ferry, on clothes-shopping for the 5'3" Muggsy Bogues

"If I ever lose my luggage, I know where to go to borrow clothes."

Mike Fratello, on the advantages the 5'7" Fratello has coaching the 5'7" Spud Webb

"When the crowd started chanting 'Dino, Dino', his parents must have felt five feet tall."

David Graf, on the Cleveland Browns' 5'7" Dino Hall receiving a standing ovation

"No—I clean giraffe ears."

Elvin Hayes, 6'11", asked if he was a basketball player

"This will be the first time the referee drops the ball."

> *Dan Issel, anticipating a jump ball between 5'10" Michael Adams and 5'3" Muggsy Bogues*

"No, ma'am, I was a jockey for a dinosaur."

> *Johnny Kerr, 6'9", on being asked if he ever played basketball*

"If you go to the movies with him, you get in for half price."

> *Johnny Kerr, on 7'2" Mark Eaton*

"Freddie Patek is the only guy in the major leagues who needs a life preserver to get into the whirlpool bath."

> *Jim Murray*

"People will look up at me and say, 'Oh, my God.' and I'll tell 'em, 'No, I'm your center.' "

> *Chuck Nevitt, on being 7'5"*

"I never worried about being adopted."

> *Chuck Nevitt, on having two brothers who were 6'7", a father who was over 6'7" and a 6-foot-tall mother*

"The club didn't mind the added weight, but it gave him two weeks to get down to his playing height."

> *Scott Ostler, on finding out Ken Griffey, Jr. showed up for camp 20 pounds heavier and 2 inches taller*

"It's better than being the biggest player in the minor leagues."

> *Fred Patek, on being the smallest player in the majors*

"He was born on June 6th, 7th, and 8th."

> *George Raveling, on 7'2" James Donaldson*

"I'm not on a ladder."

> *Willis Reed, to Jim Wergeles, Knicks' publicist, who found out that the 6'11" Reed was painting his ceiling and cautioned him not to fall off his ladder*

"Where's the rest of your goalkeeper?"

*Larry Robinson, on the Blackhawks'
5'5" goalie Darren Pang*

"I'm the only catcher in baseball who can give the pitcher his signs standing up."

Tom Shopay, on being a short catcher

"We've finally found the perfect short man."

*Dave Smith, on the Cubs' 5'8" out-
fielder Doug Dascenzo pitching two
scoreless innings in a blowout*

"He'd be great in a short series."

*Gary Smith, on 5'5" hockey player
Bobby LaLonde*

"All right, everyone—line up alphabetically according to your height."

Casey Stengel

"Pitch him low."

*Bob Swift, on pitching to midget Ed-
die Gaedel*

"They told me they were sending me a centerfielder, but instead they sent me a midget who couldn't catch a ball."

Wes Westrum, on 5'9" outfielder Don Bosch

HIGH SCHOOL

"It's like a 360-degree turnaround. I mean a 180-degree turnaround. I only went to high school."

Steve Avery, on the Braves' rise from last to first

"I never played on the high school basketball team. Too much gee-whiz bullshit and girls jumping up in their skirts with no panties on just to drive you wacky."

Bo Belinsky

"In high school, I took a little English, some science, and some hubcaps and some wheel covers."

Gates Brown

"He reminds you of a guy who took four auto-shop classes in high school. Dan could strike out four times and somehow get dirty."

Kent Hrbek, on Dan Gladden

"They've got to where they've stopped counting his no-hitters—only his perfect games."

Doug Osborne, high school coach, on his phenom David Clyde

HISTORY

"Even Napoleon had his Watergate."

Danny Ozark, on the Phillies' blowing a 15-game lead

"He'll be OK if he keeps his hand out of his shirt."

Casey Stengel, on Dan Napoleon

"They've blamed Rod for every loss in San Antonio the last two years. If they could place him in 1836, they'd blame him for the Alamo."

Mark Termini, agent for Rod Strickland, on contract problems with the San Antonio Spurs

173

"He is the only guy I know who can go 4 for 3."
Alan Bannister, on Rod Carew

"I got a big charge out of seeing Ted Williams hit. Once in a while they let me try to field some of them, which sort of dimmed my enthusiasm."
Rocky Bridges, on Ted Williams

"You just walk up there and hit it."
Hugh Duffy, baseball Hall of Famer,
explaining his hitting philosophy

"George Brett could get good wood on an aspirin."
Jim Frey

"I think that when he comes to the plate, he should only get one swing."
Greg Gagne, on Wade Boggs

"He could hit .300 with a fountain pen."
Joe Garagiola, on Stan Musial

"Charlie Gehringer is in a rut. He bats .350 on opening day and stays there all season."

Lefty Gomez

"Happiness is going 2 for 5 and seeing your average drop."

Richie Hebner

"You're asking the wrong guy. I was in a lifelong slump."

Jim Leyland, on a Pirates' hitting slump

"Moe Berg could speak eight languages, but he couldn't hit in any of them."

Ted Lyons, on the intellectual but weak-hitting Moe Berg

"I wound up, threw, and then ducked behind the mound."

Walter Masterson, on Ted Williams

"Greaseball, greaseball, greaseball. That's all I throw him, and he still hits them. He is the only player in baseball who consistently hits my grease. He sees the ball so well. I guess he can pick the dry side."

Gaylord Perry, on Rod Carew

"Because you don't get to hit in the bullpen."

Bob Uecker, on why he never had to adjust his batting stance

HOCKEY

"It's the same as what Rhett Butler said to Scarlett O'Hara."

Howard Cosell, on his reaction after the Edmonton Oilers beat the New York Islanders in the Stanley Cup finals

"I went to a fight the other night and a hockey game broke out."

Rodney Dangerfield

"I skate to where the puck is going to be, not where it has been."

Wayne Gretzky

"Half the game is mental; the other half is being mental."

Jim McKenny

"You don't have to be crazy to play hockey, but it helps."

Bob Plager

"If you take the game seriously, you go crazy anyway, so it helps if you're a bit nuts to start with because you don't waste time getting that way."

Bob Plager

"Goaltending is a normal job. Sure! How would you like it in your job if every time you made a small mistake, a red light went on over your desk and fifteen thousand people stood up and yelled at you?"

Jacques Plante

"We know that hockey is where we live, where we can best meet and overcome pain and wrong and death. Life is just a place where we spend time between games."

Fred Shero

"If you can't beat 'em in the alley, you can't beat 'em on the ice."

Conn Smythe

"Basketball is the one sport that can truly be influenced by one man. Baseball and football can't, and hockey no one understands anyway."

Pat Williams

HOME RUNS

"It's pretty bad when your family asks for passes to the game and wants to sit in the left-field bleachers."

Bert Blyleven, on possibly breaking his own record of allowing the most home runs in a season

"I dunno, my eyes were closed."

Tom Boggs, on pitch he hit for his first home run

"Rich has been kept inside the fences longer than the hostages were held in Iran."

Mike Flanagan, on why Rich Dauer was nicknamed "The Hostage"

"That must be an awful small town."

> Billy Gardner, on Darrell Brown having the nickname "Downtown" even though he hit only one home run in 591 career at-bats

"It was an insurance run, so I hit it to the Prudential Building."

> Reggie Jackson, on hitting a home run in Fenway Park

"As I remember it, the bases were loaded."

> Garry Maddox, his reaction to a grand-slam home run he hit

"I always felt just like a kid at a circus whenever I saw him hit a home run."

> Herb Pennock, on Babe Ruth home runs

"He has enough power to hit home runs in any park—including Yellowstone."

> Paul Richards, on Harmon Killebrew

"Frisch's home run was the longest in history. He kept talking about it all the way from St. Louis to Boston."

> Red Smith, on a Frankie Frisch home run

"Anything that goes that far ought to have a stewardess on it."

> Paul Splitorff, on a George Brett home run

"I was so surprised and shocked I didn't know whether to run or walk, go forward or backward."

> Tom Tischinski, on his first home run

"Between me and my roommate we've hit 400 home runs."

> Bob Uecker, on his roommate Eddie Matthews, who had 399 home runs at the time of the statement

"You don't get your first home run too often."

> Rick Wrona, reacting to his first home run

"That rare intelligence that keeps horses from betting on human beings."

George Burns, defining horse sense

"Well, I'd say I lost a few million here and there."

Cab Calloway, on betting

"No horse can go as fast as the money you bet on him."

Nate Collier

"Fortunately, my wife is understanding. When I come home from the races, she never asks any questions if I tell her I just ate a $380 hot dog."

Tim Conway

"There goes half my friends."

John Coward, after being told that as a member of the Pennsylvania Harness Commission he could no longer associate with gamblers and lowlifes

"I try to keep myself in the best of company and my horses in the worst of company."

Lenny Goodman, jockey agent

"A place where the windows clean the people."

Bob Hope, describing the racetrack

"The only man who makes money following the races is one who does it with a broom and a shovel."

Elbert Hubbard

"The horses have no agents, they don't call me in the morning to renegotiate after winning a race, they don't petition me for more oats, and they don't object to urine analysis."

Gene Klein, on going from owning the San Diego Chargers to owning horses

"There's something about the turf—tomorrow is more appealing and interesting than today."

Larry MacPhail

"The people who think they can wind up ahead of the races are everybody who has ever won a bet."
Ogden Nash

"I'd rather have a bad day on the track than a good day off it somewhere else."
Johnny Nerud

"You know horses are smarter than people. You never heard of a horse going broke betting on people."
Will Rogers

"The race is not always to the swift, not the battle to the strong, but that's the way to bet."
Damon Runyon

"Never back the horses you admire most, for the horse you admire most never wins races."
J. A. Spencer

"I just played a horse yesterday so slow that the jockey kept a diary of the trip."
Henny Youngman

"They'll get a lot more hustle out of me than if I were making $270,000."

> *Vern Maxwell, on getting a raise to $1.6 million*

"You have to get your uniform dirty. I used to use three uniforms every day. George uses three a month."

> *Pete Rose, comparing himself to George Foster*

HYPOCHONDRIACS

"Benedict may not be hurt as much as he really is."

> *Jerry Coleman, on the injured Bruce Benedict*

"If that were Chris Brown, they'd be preparing for open heart surgery."

> *Mike LaCoss, after being hit on the chest with a line drive and staying in the game*

"You never know with those psychosomatic injuries. You have to take your time with them."

Jim Palmer

IN BAD TASTE

"I'm as happy as a faggot in a submarine."

Andre Agassi, after beating Boris Becker at the French Open

"I wouldn't want to fight him. As far as he's concerned, the marquis of Queensberry is some fag hairdresser."

Jim Bouton, on former tough teammate Fred Talbot

"I've had the security of knowing I'm a proven performer."

George Brett, on two women he was involved with having had abortions

"What do the Iraqis have in common with Lisa Olsen? They've both seen Patriot missiles up close."

Victor Kiam, New England Patriots owner, making light of the sexual harassment charges Olsen brought against three Patriots players

"I called him to wish him merry Christmas, and the call took 27 minutes."

Jim Leyland, on the stuttering problem of Junior Ortiz

INJURIES

"He's incredible. If you drop a toothpick on his foot, he'll have a stress fracture."

Stan Albeck, on Bill Walton

"Back then, if you had a sore arm, the only people concerned were you and your wife. Now, it's you, your wife, your agent, your investment counselor, your stockbroker, and your publisher."

Jim Bouton

"John Wayne would have been proud of me. They got me in the foot but I went down shooting."

> *M. L. Carr, after scoring 10 points with a broken foot*

"I was just trying to get a hit off of him. Well, not *literally* off him."

> *Milt Cuyler, on a drive up the middle that hit Jack Morris on the arm*

"What is a medium collateral whatever ligament? It sounds like spaghetti with fish sauce."

> *Art Donovan, football Hall of Famer, poking fun at the injuries suffered by current players*

"The doctor told me I can't run for the rest of the season. And I can only drink Chivas Regal."

> *Jamie Easterly, on his wishful precautions for a rash on his arm*

"I called Blue Cross, but they hung up when they found out who it was."

> *Bill Fitch, after injuries decimated the Cleveland Cavaliers*

"Waking up from all my operations."

> *Tim Foley, retired Dolphins defensive back, on the best memories from his NFL career*

"It's been frozen and defrosted more than a pork chop."

> *Rick Grace, Oklahoma basketball player, on a recurring ankle injury*

"I've had all the stitches color-coded so the autopsy will be easier for everybody."

> *Dan Hampton, after his tenth knee operation*

"When he gets down in a crouch, it sounds like a bowl of Rice Krispies."

> *Greg Hibbard, on Carlton Fisk after surgery on both knees*

"When they operated on my arm, I asked them to put in Koufax's fastball. They did. But it turned out to be Mrs. Koufax."

> *Tommy John*

"I had the tendon transfer 13 years ago, so it's just now reaching puberty."

Tommy John

"My arm will be 13 this September. I think we're going to have a bar mitzvah for it. We're going to bring in Buddy Hackett, and, who knows, maybe I can get a fountain pen."

Tommy John

"Ever since they put it in, I've been getting great reception on my car radio."

Bob Kuechenberg, on a steel pin put in his right arm

"A really bad one never heals for a long time."

John Madden, on a hamstring pull

"If I sit out another year, I'll probably get the Heisman Trophy."

Tim Marshall, Notre Dame tackle, named to the 1983 preseason All-American team after sitting out all of 1982 with an injury

"You say a couple of prayers, but they are very short prayers."

> *Chris McCarron, on what goes on in a jockey's head when falling*

"No longer than that. Maybe a month and a half."

> *Junior Ortiz, asked if an injury would keep him out for six weeks*

"I knew they had to graft a new arm on him, but did they have to give him Sandy Koufax's?"

> *Pete Rose, on Tommy John's new arm*

"He said he broke it in two places; I, of course, told him to stay out of those places."

> *Steve Stone, on Jose Rijo's broken ankle*

"I don't think it will affect his mobility. Electrical storms might be a problem."

> *Jeff Torborg, on a metal plate inserted in Carlton Fisk's broken right arm*

"I made a major contribution to the Cardinals' pennant drive in 1964. I got hepatitis."
Bob Uecker

"He tells me to drink lemon juice after a hot bath, but I never can finish drinking the bath."
Bob Uecker, on a doctor's prescription for a cold

"I learned a long time ago that minor surgery is when they do the operation on someone else, not you."
Bill Walton

INK

"How do you know when you run out of invisible ink?"
Larry Andersen, asking one of his unanswerable questions

"Never argue with people who buy ink by the gallon."
Tom Lasorda

"Having Marv Throneberry play for your team is like having Willie Sutton play for your bank."

Jimmy Breslin

"My most embarrassing moment."

Bill Buckner, on being replaced by pinch-hitter Jamie Quirk

"His pitches remind me of the garbage I take out at night."

Rod Carew, on Mike Boddicker

"There was a vacancy when I left, and the owners decided to continue with it."

Happy Chandler, on being replaced by Ford Frick as baseball commissioner

"Could be that he's a nice guy when you get to know him, but why bother?"

Dizzy Dean, on Bill Terry

"He's Hitler, but he ain't gonna make no lampshade out of me."

> Dock Ellis, on Billy Hunter

"He can catch, he can throw, and he can run, but he couldn't hit me if I walked in front of him."

> Herman Franks, on Randy Hundley

"If he doesn't win over there, he should be sued for malpractice."

> Tommy John, on Tony LaRussa's managing the A's

"If it's true you learn by your mistakes, Jim Frey will be the best manager ever."

> Ron Luciano

"The only pitcher I had left was Mike Armstrong, and the reason I didn't use him was that I wanted to win the game."

> Billy Martin

"I wish I had 10 pitchers with Bo Belinksy's stuff and none with his head."

> Gene Mauch

"From Cy Young to sayonara in one season."

> *Graig Nettles, on Sparky Lyle, who won the Cy Young and then was traded a year later*

"His limitations are limitless."

> *Danny Ozark, on Mike Anderson*

"Everybody knows that Casey Stengel has forgotten more baseball than I'll ever know. That's the trouble—he's forgotten it."

> *Jimmy Piersall*

"I'm very glad to receive the Klem Award, but I'll tell you the truth—Klem hated my guts and I hated his."

> *Beans Reardon, on winning the Bill Klem award as one of baseball's top umpires*

"I used to send a taxicab to the Almanac Hotel the day he was gonna pitch. I didn't want him to get lost on the way to the stadium."

> *Babe Ruth, on George Earnshaw*

"Most valuable player from the neck down."

Eddie Stanky, on Carl Yastrzemski

"He has the personality of a tree trunk."

John Stearns, on Dave Kingman

"Son, we'd like to keep you around this season, but we're going to try to win a pennant."

Casey Stengel, to Aubrey Gatewood

"He's 19 years old, and in 10 years he's got a chance to be 29."

Casey Stengel, on the future prospects of Greg Gossen

"He calls for the curveball too much. He can't hit it, so he figures nobody else can."

Casey Stengel, on Chris Cannizzaro

"First I found it hard to catch him. Then I found it hard to hit him. And finally I found it hard to manage him."

Joe Torre, on Phil Niekro

"He has a million-dollar arm and a ten-cent head."

Alex Trevino, on Mario Soto

"He's the only man I know Dale Carnegie would hit in the mouth."

Bill Veeck, on Walter O'Malley

"There isn't enough mustard in the state of Georgia for Mr. Perez."

Dick Williams, on hot dog Pasquel Perez

INSULTS IN BASKETBALL

"That's the one with all the No Passing signs."

An Atlanta disc jockey commenting on the possibility of a highway named in honor of Dominique Wilkens

"I heard Byron Scott went to Kentucky Fried Chicken, but he couldn't buy a bucket there either."

Anonymous, referring to Byron Scott's poor shooting in the 1991 playoffs

"I pay Robey more than anyone to come to my summer basketball camp. The kids can watch him play and see for themselves what not to do."

Larry Bird, on former teammate Rick Robey

"I told him, 'Son, I couldn't understand it with you. Is it ignorance or apathy?' He said, 'Coach, I don't know and I don't care.'"

Frank Layden, on a former player

"You did great, son. You scored one more point than a dead man."

Abe Lemons, after his star player scored one point in a game

"He and Dick Motta have had some difficulties that have to be settled. If this was Lionel Simmons, it would have been a major issue; but this is Dennis Hopson."

Jerry Reynolds, Sacramento Kings' GM, on Dennis Hopson

"Jack's box score is beginning to look like his paycheck. There is a one and then a whole lot of zeroes."

Fred Roberts, at a roast for Jack Sikma

"Instead of Hakeem, I would have preferred that my return had been against a big slug like Mark Eaton."

> *Jeff Ruland, on playing against Hakeem Olajuwon in his first NBA game after a long hiatus*

"Rupp was unique. He wanted everybody to hate him—and he succeeded."

> *Bill Spivey, on legendary coach Adolph Rupp*

"The earth in L.A. moved more in one hour than Benoit Benjamin did all last season with the Clippers."

> *Peter Vecsey, comparing a Los Angeles earthquake to Benoit Benjamin's moves on the court*

"The Knicks would be smart to keep Rory as a friend—but certainly not as the point guard."

> *Peter Vecsey, on whether the Knicks should pay nice-guy point guard Rory Sparrow what he wanted*

INSULTS IN BOXING

"He's not all that bad. If you dig deep—dig real deep, dig, dig, dig, dig, dig deep, deep, go all the way to China—I'm sure you'll find there's a nice guy in there."

George Foreman, on Mike Tyson

INSULTS IN FOOTBALL

"I would rather lose a game without Tim McKyer than win one with him."

Eddie DeBartolo

"Sometimes God gives out all the physical talent and takes away the brain."

Mike Ditka, on Tim Harris

"Karras has a lot of class. And all of it is third."

Conrad Dobler, on Alex Karras

"He's so dumb, he can't spell *cat* if you spotted him the *c* and the *a*."

> *Thomas Henderson, on Terry Bradshaw*

"She could have saved herself by dressing up as a quarterback."

> *Mike Lupica, on rumors that Mark Gastineau grabbed Brigitte Nielsen and threw her down*

"If I were the NFL commissioner, I'd put all the offensive linemen in jail for 30 days or make them spend one week with Mike Ditka."

> *Dexter Manley*

"Jim has the Midas touch—everything he touches turns to mufflers."

> *Steve Raible, on Washington State coach Jim Walden*

"Al Davis is the kind of guy who would steal your eyes and then try to convince you that you looked better without them."

> *Sam Rutigliano*

"Drop me a note if you find somebody who likes this guy, will you?"

> Sam Wyche, on Jerry Glanville

"He does the work of three men—Larry, Curley, and Moe."

> Vic Ziegel, on Ed Garvey, the NFL union negotiator

INSULTS IN TENNIS

"Because John McEnroe never played it."

> Larry Felser, on why so many millions of people love pro football

INSULTS IN TRACK AND FIELD

"The only thing that is amateur about track and field is its organization."

> Craig Masback

"I don't have one bad memory from my 13 seasons. I don't have a memory at all, for that matter."

Bubba Baker, on his NFL career

"The guys tell me I have nothing to protect—no brain, no pain."

Randy Carlyle, on why he is one of the few hockey players who does not wear a helmet

"The good Lord was good to me. He gave me a strong body, a good right arm, and a weak mind."

Dizzy Dean

"The doctors x-rayed my head and found nothing."

Dizzy Dean

"The shoulder surgery was a success. The lobotomy failed."

Mike Ditka, on Jim McMahon's off-season surgery

"Physically, he's a world beater. Mentally, he's an egg beater."

Matt Elliott, on former Ohio State linebacker Alonzo Spellman

"That's so when I forget how to spell my name, I can still find my clothes."

Stu Grimson, on the Chicago Blackhawks' decision to display color pictures of each player above their locker

"Phil Jackson is one of the most intelligent players I ever saw. He's so smart he can commit 12 fouls and only get caught for 4."

Red Holtzman

"Albert Einstein was bad in English; of course, Einstein was German."

Bob Kearney, defending his own intelligence

"It was awful. Everybody knew I was the dumbest one in the room."

Frank Layden, after giving a speech at Harvard Law School

"**I**'m intelligent enough to read William F. Buckley's column, but I'm not intellectual enough to finish it."

> *Marv Levy, on having a history degree from Harvard*

"**W**e're more aggressive, more mobile, and more smarter."

> *Greg Lloyd, Steelers' linebacker, on why the Steelers had better linebackers than the Bears*

"**I** don't understand the questions of things he can answer."

> *Ed Lynch, on Yale grad Ron Darling*

"**I**t's better to be quiet and ignorant than to open your mouth and remove all doubt."

> *John McNamara*

"**M**ike Ivie is a $40 million airport with a $30 control tower."

> *Rick Monday*

"Oh, yeah. I remember him—short guy, mustache, plays third base for Pittsburgh."

> *Jackie Moore, on being on the same plane as economist John Kenneth Galbraith*

"We were the quintessence of athletic atrocity."

> *Mike Newlin, after a New York Nets loss*

"I'll tell you how smart Pete is. When they had the blackout in New York, he was stranded 13 hours on an escalator."

> *Joe Nuxhall, on Pete Rose*

"Not if I had to have his brain too."

> *Bob Ojeda, asked if he wanted Randy Myers's fastball*

"They could play me at third. They have to have my brain in there somewhere."

> *Junior Ortiz, after being replaced as the Twins' backup catcher*

"He didn't sound like a baseball player. He said things like 'Nevertheless,' and 'If, in fact.' "
                            Dan Quisenberry, on Ted Simmons

"A lot of little broads and a jazz band."
                            Mayo Smith, on what you would find
                            if you opened a baseball player's head

"I know a lot of people think I'm dumb. Well, at least I ain't no educated fool."
                            Leon Spinks

"He's a quick learner, but he forgets quick too."
                            Mychal Thompson, on Vlade Divac

"Ninety percent of the game is half mental."
                            Jim Wohlford, on baseball

INTERCEPTIONS

"I hope one of my senior quarterbacks is drawn, so the pie will be intercepted before it gets to my face."

> *Gary Fallon, Washington and Lee football coach, on a drawing to determine which player will throw a pie in his face for charity*

INTERVIEWS

"Spuds Mackenzie is a better interview than Rickey Henderson."

> *Ron Kittle*

"No comment."

> *Doug Moe, on being asked what he thought of being named coach of the NBA all-interview team*

"That's like giving Charles Manson the keys to the city."

> *Mike Smithson, on Dennis Boyd's being given a chain saw as a gift for a TV interview*

I Q

"Out of what—a thousand?"
> *Mickey Rivers, on Reggie Jackson's claims that he has a 160 IQ*

"When I got on the team bus, she flashed me her IQ number."
> *Jerry Sloan, on being taunted by Dennis Rodman and his wife*

"When you tackle Campbell, it reduces your IQ."
> *Pete Wysocki, on Earl Campbell*

JEWELRY

"What's that, a Mr. T starter set?"
> *Mike Diaz, on the three gold chains around Vincent Palacios's neck*

"After all these years wearing 29, I imagine Barfield has quite a bit of jewelry invested in that number."
> *Dave LaPoint, on giving up number 29 to Jesse Barfield*

"They got guys playing today with earrings in their ear. If I was still pitching, I'd throw one in their earring."

Billy Loes

"He treats us like men. He lets us wear earrings."

Torrin Polk, Houston receiver, on why he likes his coach

JOBS

"It's just a job. Grass grows, birds fly, waves pound the sand. I beat people up."

Muhammad Ali

"The war will be over in two weeks. That will make it the longest that Luke ever had a real job."

Mrs. Luke Appling, after her husband was drafted in World War II

"My ultimate dream is to have my own bank, maybe in Paris. I'd call it Banks's Bank on the Left Bank."

Ernie Banks

"I didn't want any phone calls at 4 A.M. from people crying, 'Fifi is throwing up.'"

> *Doug Bogue, Kansas State quarterback, who switched his major from veterinary medicine to petroleum geology*

"I would rather he was a dustman [trash collector] or a road sweeper than a professional boxer."

> *Joe Bugner, on his son's decision to become a boxer*

"Every 40 years I change jobs."

> *Ellis Clary, on leaving a scouting job with the Twins to work for the White Sox*

"The two most important jobs in America are held by foreigners—room service and field-goal kicking."

> *Beano Cook*

"In my next life, I want to play another position. I want a different job. I want to own my own business, a stress-free job. Maybe I'll grow worms and sell them."

> *Kevin Duckworth*

"Ellis, I'm impressed. You're doing the work of two men—Laurel and Hardy."

Calvin Griffith, to Ellis Clary

"The really scary thing is that some of those people work for the government."

Joe Jacoby, on Redskins fans who show up for the game with pig snouts

"To me football is like a day off. I grew up picking cotton on my daddy's farm, and nobody asked for your autograph or put your name in the paper for that."

Lee Roy Jordan

"If I had a two-hour job a day, I don't see how you can't be focused. I mean, this is a job."

Harold Katz, owner of the Philadelphia 76ers

"I'm a vice president in charge of special marketing. That means I play golf and go to cocktail parties. I'm pretty good at my job."

Mickey Mantle

"I have a darn good job with the Cardinals, but please don't ask me what I do."

Stan Musial

"I'm proud of my sons and happy they don't have to work for a living."

> *Phil Niekro, Sr., on his baseball-playing sons, Phil and Joe*

"These are the games that make you want to sell insurance."

> *Tom Olivadotti, Dolphins' defensive coordinator, after the Bills got 583 yards of offense against the Dolphins*

"It makes as much sense as a secretary going home and spending nights typing."

> *Walter Payton, on why he doesn't watch "Monday Night Football"*

"A new broom sweeps clean, but it takes an old one to get into the corners."

> *Sam Rutigliano, after losing his job at age 53*

"My conscience hurt me. I hate to play golf when I should be out working, so the only thing to do was quit working."

> *Jim Umbracht, former major leaguer, on why he quit his off-season job as ticket salesman for the Houston Colts*

"It's like a nervous breakdown with a weekly pay-check."

> *Pat Williams, describing his job as GM of the Orlando Magic*

"I can't. They both want raises."

> *Glenn Wilson, owner of a gas station, who was told to pay more attention to his hitting mechanics*

KING KONG

"If me and King Kong went into an alley, only one of us would come out, and it wouldn't be the monkey."

> *Lyle Alzado*

"We play like King Kong one day and like Fay Wray the next."

> *Terry Kennedy, on the inconsistent play of the Padres*

"The last time I saw a guy that strong, he was hanging onto the Empire State Building with Fay Wray in his arms."

> *Tom Paciorek, on Pete Incaviglia*

LANGUAGE

"It's a good language to have, because if I meet an ancient Roman, just think of the great conversation I can have with him."

John Garret, former NHL goalie, on why he taught himself Latin

LAW AND ORDER

"I'm not a public defender. I'm not a marriage counselor or an auto mechanic."

Sandy Alderson, A's GM, on his reaction to Jose Canseco's being charged with ramming his wife's car

"He would play a convicted rapist if he could turn the double play."

Jim Bouton, on Leo Durocher

"He's the only guy we had who looked like Judge Wapner."

> Dave LaPoint, on why the 45-year-old Tommy John was put in charge of the Yankees' Kangaroo Court

"Ben Johnson must still be the fastest human in the world. He served a lifetime sentence in only two years."

> Mike Littwin, Baltimore Sun writer, after Johnson's lifetime ban was lifted in two years

"I should have told them about the color TV and the Steinway piano I always carry."

> David Magley, Cleveland Cavaliers forward, who received a $1,000 check after his hotel room was burglarized

"They must have been an expansion gang."

> Gene Mauch, on hearing about a gang war in which one gang had faulty ammunition

"The last time I smiled so much was for a jury."

> Pasquel Perez, after posting his fourth victory in a row

"We were the only team in pro football whose team picture showed both a front and side view."

Ken Stabler, on the Oakland Raiders

LAWYERS

"The best description of utter waste would be for a busload of lawyers to go over a cliff with three empty seats."

Lamar Hunt

"I signed Oscar Gamble on the advice of my attorney. I no longer have Oscar Gamble, and I no longer have my attorney."

Ray Kroc, late owner of the San Diego Padres

"I lived down here for eight years and never did pass a bar."

Dick Williams, on hearing that Tony LaRussa passed the Florida bar exam

LAZINESS

"It's a lot tougher to get up in the mornings when you start wearing silk pajamas."

Eddie Arcaro

"Buddy says the two biggest career shorteners are hustle and sweat. Oh, Buddy hustles—but he hustles at his own pace. He's a slow hustler. The biggest thing Buddy does all winter is renew his subscription to *TV Guide*."

Rich Donnelly, on Buddy Bell

LEFTIES

"What do you expect in a northpaw world?"

Bill Lee, on why southpaws are always flaky

"You have a left and a right. The left side controls the right half of your body, and the right side controls the left half. Therefore left-handers are the only people in their right mind."

Bill Lee

"There ain't a left-hander in the world who can run a straight line. It's the gravitational pull on the axis of the earth that gets 'em."

Ray Miller

"Left-handers have more enthusiasm for life. They sleep on the wrong side of the bed, and their heads get more stagnant on that side."

Casey Stengel

LEGENDS

"Was Robin Hood's mother known as Mother Hood?"

Larry Andersen, asking another one of his unanswerable questions

"All the lies about him are true."

Joe Dugan, on Babe Ruth

"I might trade them if I was offered Sandy Koufax and Babe Ruth, but they're dead. Well, Sandy isn't dead, but his arm is."

Whitey Herzog, on the value of Chuck Finley and Jim Abbott to the Angels

"I want to go down in immortality."

> *Larry Holmes, on why he wanted to pass Rocky Marciano's undefeated record as a boxer*

"This is like Orville Wright coming back and deciding to run United Airlines."

> *Stan Jones, on Bears' owner George Halas's decision to get more involved with the club*

"I know I'm old, fat, and ugly, but I'm still Ted Williams."

> *Ted Williams, after a security guard didn't recognize him at a Red Sox benefit*

LITERATURE

"Yeah, what paper you write for, Ernie?"

> *Yogi Berra, on meeting Ernest Hemingway*

"He's the only guy in history who has played both Hamlet and Portland."

> Carnie Edison, on Paul Westhead, Shakespearean scholar and basketball coach

"For you readers of English descent, I'll be back in a fortnight."

> Joe Magrane

LITTLE LEAGUE

"I bet you don't know what is the first thing Little Leaguers always ask me: 'How much money do you make?'"

> Rocky Bridges

"I've lost enough weight at various times to put together an entire Little League team."

> Bubba Paris

"He struck out three times and lost the game when a ball went through his legs. Parents swore at us and threw things at our car as we left the parking lot. Gosh, I was proud. A chip off the old block."

Bob Uecker, on his son's Little League experience

"Little League is a disaster. It exists for parents who are trying vicariously to remember an ability of their own that never really existed."

Bill Veeck

"For the parents of a Little Leaguer, a baseball game is simply a nervous breakdown divided into innings."

Earl Wilson

LOSING

"You know your team's not in the race when guys are growing beards for the duck hunting season."

Steve Boros

"I was 1–9, with any luck I'd have been 2–7."

Jim Bouton, on playing for an expansion team in the Mexican League

"If a tie is like kissing your sister, losing is like kissing your grandmother with her teeth out."

George Brett

"The depth of his frown is in direct proportion to the length of his losing streak."

Jim Brosnan, on Fred Hutchinson

"My fellow coaches liked me. They were always glad to see me—as long as I brought my team with me."

P. J. Carlesimo

"I hate to lose more than I love to win. I hate to see the happiness in their faces when they beat me."

Jimmy Connors

"It was a building year, but the building caved in on me."

Nick Coso, on his 0–8 record at Ferris State

"I'd never been to a mercy killing before."

Benny Dees, New Orleans coach, after his team lost to Alabama 101–76

"We're the only team in history that could lose nine games in a row and then go into a slump."

> *Bill Fitch, on a bad Cleveland Cavaliers team*

"Last year wasn't all that bad. We led the league in flu shots."

> *Bill Fitch, on that same bad Cavaliers team*

"I'll tell you what trouble is. It's when your admissions director, who is an alumnus of your opponent, sits on the opposite side of the field for the game and not with your own fans."

> *Vic Gatto, Tufts coach, on a 0–7–1 season*

"I think the whole game hinged on one call—the one I made last April scheduling the game."

> *Peter Gavett, women's basketball coach at Maine, after his team lost to Virginia 115–57*

"We lost 13 straight one year. I decided if we got rained out, we'd have a victory party."

> *Lefty Gomez, on his minor league managing days*

"My players knew that under NCAA rules they can take one day off a week, but why'd they have to pick Saturday?"

> *John Gutekunst, Minnesota football coach, after losing to Colorado 58–0*

"We're waiting on a bid from the NIT."

> *Dick Harter, coach of the Charlotte Hornets, after they won only their 20th game in mid-April*

"Things got so bad that I had to play my student manager for a while. Things got really bad when she started to complain to the press that she wasn't getting enough playing time."

> *Linda Hill-McDonald, Minnesota women's basketball coach, after a 6–22 season*

"At Arkansas, they made a stamp to commemorate you; then, after last year, they had to stop making it because people were spitting on the wrong side."

> *Lou Holtz*

"We never had to practice kicking off."

> Tunch Ilkin, on the benefits of the
> Steelers' not scoring a touchdown in
> four weeks

"I'd rather be a football coach. That way you only lose 11 games a year."

> Abe Lemons, college basketball coach

"Last night I sat down and tried to think about the highlights from last year and I fell asleep."

> Tom Lovatt, Utah football coach, after
> a 1–10 season

"Losing streaks are funny. If you lose at the beginning, you get off to a bad start. If you lose in the middle of the season, you're in a slump. If you lose at the end, you're choking."

> Gene Mauch

"The only difference between the Mets and the *Titanic* is that the Mets have a better organist."

> Jim Murray, on a bad Mets team

"Last season we couldn't win at home, and this season we can't win on the road. My failure as a coach is that I can't think of anyplace else to play."

> Harry Neale, coach of the Vancouver Canucks

"It's not whether you win or lose but who gets the blame."

> Blaine Nye

"Sure, on a given day I could beat him—but it would have to be a day he had food poisoning."

> Mel Purcell, after losing to Ivan Lendl in 58 minutes

"It's tough. Neither of us go into a restaurant around here, but for different reasons."

> Jerry Reynolds, Sacramento GM and native of French Lick, Indiana, the same hometown as Larry Bird, after having supper with Bird

"I zigged when I should have zagged."

> Jack Roper, after recovering from a knockout by Joe Louis

"It was like taking Miss America home after a date and discovering that she had just won a garlic-eating contest."

> Blackie Sherrod, after the NCAA took away Florida's first-ever football title

"When my ship comes in, there will be a dock strike."
> Gene Ubriaco, after his AHL team lost 21 games in a row

"The only difference between me and General Custer is that I had to watch the films on Sunday."
> Rick Venturi, Northwestern football coach, after losing to Ohio State 63–20

LOTTERY

"She is now."

> Chuck Tanner, asked if his aunt who won $2.5 million in a lottery was his favorite aunt

"I'm not disloyal. I'm the most loyal player money can buy."

Don Sutton, on being a free agent

LUGE

"It was what I would call the ultimate laxative."

Otto Jelinek, Canada's minister of sports, after taking a luge run in Calgary

LYING

"I've got one fault. I lie a lot."
Tom Lasorda

"I don't want to tell you any half-truths unless they're completely accurate."

> Dennis Rappaport, on Tommy Hearns

"I didn't want to win it this way, but I can always lie to my grandchildren."

> Mike Swain, U.S. Olympic judo team member who was awarded a bronze medal after the third-place finisher was disqualified

MAGAZINES

"I told them the only way they could lose credibility quicker would be to put me in the swimsuit issue."

> Lou Holtz, on preseason polls that ranked a bad Notre Dame team in the Top 20

"It's the only time in my life that my wife let me buy the magazine."

> Don James, on why he was glad his star tackle made the Playboy All-American Team

"The phone rang and my wife told me it was *Sports Illustrated.* I cut myself shaving and fell down the steps in my rush to get to the phone. I said hello and a voice on the other end said, 'For just 75 cents an issue. . . .' "

> *Speedy Morris, basketball coach at LaSalle, on what he thought would be his first major interview*

"LaRoche is like the *Sporting News.* He comes out once a week."

> *Graig Nettles, on Dave LaRoche's being sent up and down between the minors and major leagues*

MALAPROPS AND FRACTURED SYNTAX

"Our similarities are different."
> *Dale Berra, on his father*

"No, but he did a lot better than I thought he would."
> *Yogi Berra, on whether Don Mattingly exceeded expectations in 1984*

"I really didn't say everything I said."
        Yogi Berra

"That's his style of hitting. If you can't imitate him, don't copy him."
        Yogi Berra, on Frank Robinson's hitting style

"You observe a lot just by watching."
        Yogi Berra

"Rich Folkers is throwing up in the bullpen."
        Jerry Coleman

"If Pete Rose brings the Reds in, they ought to bronze him and put him in cement."
        Jerry Coleman, on what would happen if Rose led the Reds to the World Series

"Young Frank Pastore may have pitched the biggest game of 1979—maybe the biggest victory of the year."
        Jerry Coleman

"McCovey swings and misses, and it's fouled back."
Jerry Coleman

"He slides into second with a stand-up double."
Jerry Coleman

"Most of our future lies ahead."
Denny Crum

"The runners have returned to their respectable bases."
Dizzy Dean

"Bruce Sutter has been around a while, and he's pretty old. He's 35 years old. That will give you an idea of how old he is."
Ron Fairly

"I must have had ambrosia."
Jim Gantner, on missing a radio show appearance

"Hey, this isn't over until they beat us tomorrow."
Cito Gaston, the day before the Blue Jays lost to the Twins

"I saw that kid play at Wisconsin Rapids last year. I knew immediately he was doomed to become an all-star outfielder."

Calvin Griffith, on Jim Eisenreich

"The Mets have gotten their leadoff batter on base only once in this inning."

Ralph Kiner

"The reasons the Mets have played so well at Shea this season is that they have the best home record in baseball."

Ralph Kiner

"Jose DeLeon on his career has a record of 73 wins and 105 RBIs."

Ralph Kiner

"Sutton lost 13 games in a row without winning a ball game."

Ralph Kiner

"Tony Gwynn was named player of the year for April."

Ralph Kiner

"He's got a whole new set of banisters."

Don King, on Mike Tyson's attorneys

"No fuckin' way. You've all gotta be there."

Moose Lallo, International League hockey coach, asked if a practice was mandatory

"I'd like to be sort of like Lou Boudreau. He does a good job of recapping the play before it happens."

Johnny Logan

"I'll have to go with the immoral Babe Ruth."

Johnny Logan, asked to name the greatest player ever

"It's not so much maturity as it is growing up."

Jay Miller, hockey player, asked if his improved play was due to maturity

"I've got a great repertoire with my players."

Danny Ozark

"It's beyond my apprehension."

Danny Ozark, on a Phillies' losing streak

"Morality at this point isn't a factor."

Danny Ozark, on the Phillies' morale during a losing streak

"Don't you guys think for a minute that I'm going to take this loss standing down."

Bill Petersen, former Houston Oilers coach

"Three things are bad for you. I can't remember the first two, but doughnuts are the third."

Bill Petersen

"But I'm getting better since I took up that Sam Carnegie course."

Bill Petersen, admitting to frequent use of malaprops

"We'll do all right if we can capitalize on our mistakes."

Mickey Rivers

"My goals are to hit .300, score 100 runs, and stay injury prone."

Mickey Rivers

"I'm going to cancel my prescription."

Bob Stanley, after being criticized in a Boston paper

"There comes a time in every man's life, and I've had plenty of them."

Casey Stengel

"I want to thank all my players for giving me the honor of being what I was."

Casey Stengel

"He immediately got rid of the ball quickly."

Hank Stram

"He lived to fight. Even if he didn't get paid for it, he'd still want a fight just to release the monopoly."

Chuck Wergeles, on boxer Beau Jack

"It would prove a test of whether there are any repercussions in his arm."

> Wes Westrum, on a pitcher's return after an injury

"Winfield robbed Armas of at least a home run."

> Bill White, on Dave Winfield's leap into the stands to rob Tony Armas of a home run

MANAGERS AND MANAGING

"There are three things the average man thinks he can do better than everybody else: build a fire, run a motel, and manage a baseball team."

> Rocky Bridges

"My wife doesn't have to buy shoes at a garage sale anymore."

> Doc Edwards, former major league manager and coach, on being asked the difference between managing and coaching

"I like playing for Dick, but once I get out of the game, I'm going to run over him with a car."

Tim Flannery, on Dick Williams

"They say most good managers were mediocre players. I should be a helluva manager."

Charlie Hough

"When I first became a manager, I asked Chuck for advice. He told me, 'Always rent.'"

Tony LaRussa, on what he learned from Chuck Tanner

"He was like a college professor. I thought he had tenure."

Mike Macfarlane, on finding out that Bobby Valentine was fired after eight years as the Texas Rangers manager

"Joe Altobelli tried to treat the players like men, but it's well known most ballplayers are a bunch of asses."

Bill Madlock

"The toughest thing about managing is standing up for nine innings."

Paul Owens

"The secret of managing a club is to keep the five guys who hate you from the five who are undecided."
     Casey Stengel

"I'm not sure whether I'd rather be managing or testing bulletproof vests."
          Joe Torre, on enduring a nine-game losing streak when managing the Mets

"I asked her how she would like to be married to a big-league manager, and she said, 'You mean Tommy Lasorda is getting a divorce?' "
          John Wathan, on how he informed his wife he was becoming a manager

"If he had made me a consultant five minutes ago, my first recommendation would have been not to fire the manager."
          John Wathan, on being offered a job as a consultant after being fired by the Kansas City Royals

"Only if I had one year to live."
          Mookie Wilson, asked if he wanted to manage in the big leagues

"I like my players to be married and in debt. That's the way you motivate them."
Ernie Banks

"I don't want nobody who looks worse than me."
Richard Dent, on his marriage plans

"We were happily married for eight months. Unfortunately, we were married for four and a half years."
Nick Faldo, on his ex-wife

"Last year was a honeymoon. This year has been a marriage."
Bob Hill, Indiana Pacers coach, after a great rookie year and a tough second year

"My wife, Beth, and I have a little trouble communicating. When I say 'broad,' she thinks about a trip to Europe. When she says 'diamond,' I think of baseball."
Lou Holtz

"Playing for Billy Martin is like being married to him. Right now we're all sleeping on the couch."

Matt Keough

"He caused me a lot of aggravation, he taught me to play golf, and he introduced me to my wife."

Dave Leonhard, on why he doesn't talk to his old friend Jim Palmer

"I met my wife in a New York bar. We had a lot in common: we were both from California, and we were both drunk."

Tug McGraw

"No, sir, but I'm in great demand."

Satchel Paige, asked if he was married

"I really don't know. I don't see her that much."

Ray Perkins, on how his wife felt about his 18-hour work days at Alabama

"It's a marriage. If I had to choose between my wife and my putter—well, I'd miss her."

> Gary Player, on the putter he has used since 1967

"When my wife said, 'I do.'"

> Dick Vitale, on the biggest surprise of his life

MEANNESS

"Seriously, coach Lombardi is very fair. He treats us all like dogs."

> Henry Jordan, on Vince Lombardi

"He turned his life around. He used to be depressed and miserable. Now he's miserable and depressed."

> Harry Kalas, on Garry Maddox

"Munson's not moody, he's just mean. When you're moody, you're nice sometimes."

> Sparky Lyle, on Thurman Munson

"Sweet refers to his swing, not his personality."
Phil Rizzuto, on Lou Piniella

"All that jumping around, tipping their hats, shaking hands with the fans—I might knock down more of them today than I did when I pitched. I wouldn't waste a pitch hitting 'em either. I'd hit 'em in the dugout."
Early Wynn, on players who take curtain calls after home runs

MEDIA

"It puts Jose Canseco three weeks behind in bad publicity."
Buddy Baron, on the affects of the three-week spring-training lockout

"When I can't make up my mind about changing a pitcher or putting in a pinch hitter, I listen for ideas the announcer has, then do the opposite."
Ben Chapman, asked why he listened to a radio in the dugout

"He never remembered a sign or forgot a newspaper-man's name."

Leo Durocher, on Ernie Banks

"If Chris was broadcasting World War II, he'd thank the Japanese for coming and invite them back."

Ed Fowler, on nice-guy sportscaster Chris Schenkel

"The only way to get along with newspapermen is to be like Dizzy Dean: say something one minute and something different the next."

Hank Greenberg

"He'd give you the shirt off his back. Of course, he'd call a press conference to announce it."

Jim Hunter, on Reggie Jackson

"I believe every person was put on Earth for a reason. Mine was to sell newspapers."

Eric Lindros

"I can't rationalize talking to press people because they're not rational people."

John McEnroe

"The perfect Christmas gift for sportscasters, as all
fans of sports clichés know, is a scoreless tie."
William Safire

"By the next morning it is a shroud for obsolete
haddock."
Red Smith, on the importance of the
sports page

MEDIOCRITY

"The more I played with them, the more I found that
no one could take a joke—my batting average."
Rocky Bridges, on batting .237 for the
Dodgers

"If I did anything funny on the ballfield, it was strictly
accidental. Like the way I played third. Some people
thought it was hilarious, but I was on the level all the
time."
Rocky Bridges

"We're like a hockey team. We play in shifts. And I'm still driving the Zamboni."

> Dave Collins, on constant Reds' lineup changes

"The one thing that kept Jack Perconte from being a good major-league player is performance."

> Del Crandall

"When you hear the fans saying good luck to you, you know you're in trouble."

> Jerry Dybzinski

"I went through life as a 'player to be named later.'"

> Joe Garagiola

"I'm scared. I think I'm the best player here."

> Scott Hastings, on the Miami Heat, an expansion team

"Baseball has been good to me since I quit trying to play it."

> Whitey Herzog

"My biggest thrill came the night Elgin Baylor and I combined for 73 points in Madison Square Garden. Elgin had 71 of them."

> *Hot Rod Hundley*

"Give them time. They'll learn."

> *Rich Kelly, after being given a standing ovation by Phoenix Suns fans after he was traded there*

"It was the same story every place I went. I was the guy they kept for insurance. They should have dressed me in a policy instead of a uniform."

> *Jack Kemp, on his early pro football days*

"I thought I did until I looked at some old game films."

> *Bum Phillips, asked if he played college football*

"When the year was over they wanted to give me back as the player to be named later."

> *Richie Scheinblum, after he was traded from Cleveland to Washington for cash and a player to be named later*

"The Dodgers are such a .500 club, they could probably split a three-game series."

Vin Scully, on the 1990 Dodgers

"What does Alston think I am—a machine?"

Dick Stuart, after starting three straight games for the Dodgers

"I'm in the twilight of a mediocre career."

Frank Sullivan

"Why am I wasting so much dedication on a mediocre career?"

Ron Swoboda

"Because the teams are spending fortunes and playing .500."

Syd Thrift, on calling the American League East the Fortune 500

"The highlight of my career? Oh, I'd say that was in 1967 in St. Louis. I walked with the bases loaded to drive in the winning run in an intersquad game in spring training."

Bob Uecker

"You know I signed with the Milwaukee Braves for $3,000. That bothered my dad at the time, because he didn't have that kind of dough to pay out. But eventually he scraped it up."
Bob Uecker

"Anybody with ability can play in the big leagues. But to be able to trick people year in and year out the way I did—I think that's a much greater feat."
Bob Uecker

"He looked like Bobby Orr out there. Some nights, however, he looks like iron ore."
Tom Webster, on an exciting goal by defenseman Rob Blake

"Most players are born to hit. I was born to hit .238."
Don Zimmer

MINORS

"I've been to every baseball park in America except those in the American and National League."
Rich Amaral, career minor leaguer, who made the majors at age 30

"When I was a kid I used to pray to the Lord to make me a hockey player. Unfortunately, I forgot to mention the NHL, and so I spent 16 years in the minors.
Don Cherry

"I hate the minor leagues. I'd rather go out to lunch with my ex-wife's attorney than play in the minors."
Dave Collins

"Sometimes I think the CBA is there only to give you the inspiration to get out of there."
Milt Newton

"In the minors, I stayed in the hotels where the fire escape was a rope."
Tony Torchia, Red Sox coach, on coaching 25 years in the minors

"We didn't have a team bus. We had a team bike."
Johnny Unitas, on his days with a semipro team

"The biggest adjustment from the minor leagues to the major leagues is learning how to spend $45 in meal money a day."
Andy Van Slyke

"There are fewer bugs in my apartment."
   *Jim Walewander, on the difference
   between the majors and the minors*

M O M

"I know their mother—she'd give them all my plays."
   *Bobby Bowden, on why he refuses to
   play against his sons, who are both
   college coaches*

"I never did say that you can't be a nice guy and win.
I said that if I was playing third base and my mother
rounded third with the winning run, I'd trip her up."
   Leo Durocher

"I've been sleeping with his mother."
   *Dick Leach, USC tennis coach, on how
   he recruited his son for the USC tennis team*

"I'd run over Grimm's mother, too."
   *Matt Millen, when told that Russ
   Grimm would run over his own
   mother to win Super Bowl XVII*

251

"Mother wanted to make sure I brushed my teeth after every meal."

> Don Sutton, explaining a phone call
> after his first victory

"When I played baseball, I got death threats all the time—from my mother."

> Bob Uecker

"Don't forget—Mother was a hell of a hitter."

> Early Wynn, on stories that he was so
> mean that he wouldn't give his
> mother a good pitch to hit

MONEY

"Give him a couple of million. He shouldn't have to take a second job to support himself or anything."

> Jose Canseco, on why Rob Dibble
> should earn more than $200,000 a
> year

"Ask for $35 million for five years. Then you and I will start our own league."

> Jose Canseco, on what Bobby Bonilla
> should ask for as a free agent

"As men get older, the toys get more expensive."

> Marvin Davis, on buying the Oakland
> A's for $12 million

"I'm independently wealthy. I have enough money to last me the rest of my life—provided I die tomorrow."
Bill Fitch

"The question isn't at what age I want to retire—it's at what income."

> George Foreman

"Not unless a key is missing on the typewriter."

> Dave Hannan, asked if he expected to
> get a million dollars in salary arbitra-
> tion

"People think we make $3 million and $4 million a year. They don't realize that most of us only make $500,000."

> Pete Incaviglia

"All I know is that if Sandy Koufax was pitching today, he wouldn't be able to count the money he'd be getting—he'd have to weigh it."

Tommy Lasorda

"They say that money talks, but the only thing it ever said to me was good-bye."

Joe Louis

"Forecheck, backcheck, paycheck."

Gil Perreault, on the secret of success in the NHL

"We don't supply women, so it must be money."

Bum Phillips, asked if Dennis Winston was holding out over money

"Earl Campbell ain't like those high-priced spoiled athletes. Why, he had me over to his office the other day just like one of the guys."

Bum Phillips, on being Earl Campbell's coach

"Yeah. At the bank."

> *Jim Rice, asked during an injury-plagued season if there was one place he was not hurting*

"Look for a rate hike."

> *Bill Russell, refusing to reveal how much he got paid for a telephone commercial*

"If I had a dollar for every time someone asked me that question . . . wait a minute—I *do* have a dollar for every time I've been asked that question."

> *Scott Skiles, on being asked about his decision to attend Michigan State over Indiana and a recent $8.4 million contract signing*

"One year I hit .291 and had to take a salary cut. If you hit .291 today, you own the franchise."

> *Enos Slaughter*

"Man, if I made $1 million, I would be in at 6 in the morning, sweep the stands, wash the uniforms, clean out the offices, manage the team, and play the game."

> *Duke Snider*

"I'll fight him for nothing if the price is right."

Marlon Starling, on a proposed match against Lloyd Honeyghan

"If I want to meet millionaires, all I have to do is visit my locker room."

George Steinbrenner, on declining an invitation to a luncheon with a group of millionaires

"If I was playing today, I'd be a million-dollar player. Is that scary or what?"

Bob Uecker, in 1992

"Just have them meet me on the first or the 15th of the month. Then there will be no doubt which Valvano is which."

Bob Valvano, coach at Kutztown State, asked if he was ever confused with brother Jim

"In here, it ought to be W-4-million forms."

Andy Van Slyke, on IRS W-4 forms that were being passed around the Pirates' clubhouse

"He could recite almost every line of *The Wizard of Oz* in all those cute little voices."

> *Margo Adams, discussing the cute*
> *traits of Wage Boggs*

"You should see the last 15 minutes of the movie. I couldn't even see it."

> *Yogi Berra, on* Fatal Attraction

"Oh, what's the matter with you now?"

> *Yogi Berra, to his wife after she saw*
> *Dr. Zhivago*

"Only one 20-year-old was ever worth making a movie about. That was Mozart."

> *Bill Bradley, on John Drew, who*
> *wanted to make a movie about his life*
> *at the age of 20*

"Howard's making a movie. It's called *The Summer of 4 to 3*."

> *Clint Hurdle, on Howard Johnson's propensity for grounding out to the second baseman*

"He's no-nonsense. He just gets after it. He's there to win. That's a lot like me. He walks the walk, he talks the talk. He's a Dirty Harry. Just call me Dirty Larry."

> *Larry Johnson, on why his idol is Clint Eastwood*

"Only if Brooke Shields would play Jane."

> *Steve Lundquist, Olympic swimmer, asked if he wanted to play Tarzan in the movies*

"Having him on the power play is like putting Cheryl Tiegs at middle linebacker."

> *Eric Nesterenko, on working with Rob Lowe in the movie* Youngblood

"They think they're hockey goalies."
> Patrick Roy, goalie for the Montreal
> Canadiens, on why his kids are not
> scared by bad guys in horror movies

"Boxing is a great exercise—as long as you can yell 'cut' whenever you want to."
> Sylvester Stallone

"Dedmon, don't wear plaid."
> Ted Turner, to pitcher Jeff Dedmon
> wearing a plaid jacket in a hotel lobby

MOVING

"I wanted to be like Larry Brown. I walked like him. I talked like him. I even moved four times."
> Billy Crystal

"I've got the kind of furniture that when you snap your fingers, it jumps into the crate."
> Jerry Glanville, on his many moves in
> 20 years of coaching

"Even his perspiration has muscles."
Jimmy Foxx, on Ted Kluszewski

"He had muscles in his hair."
Lefty Gomez, on Jimmy Foxx

MUSIC

"Whatever Jim Rice wants."
Roger Clemens, on the music the Red Sox listen to on the team bus

"I go to the locker room and the kids have headphones. They say they're listening to ZZ Topp. What ever happened to the Four Tops?"
Jimmy Connors

"I like it because it plays old music."
Tug McGraw, on his '54 Buick

"**W**ho is she?"

*Casey Weldon, Florida State quarter-
back, on being told he was going to sit
next to Ringo Starr at the Grammy
Awards*

MYTHOLOGY

"**T**he best thing about him is that he's built like a
Greek goddess."

Sparky Anderson, on Jose Canseco

"**H**e's got a body like a Greek god and the running
ability of a Greek goddess."

Dick Vitale, on George McGinnis

NAMES

"**M**y wife calls me 'Much-Maligned.' She thinks that's
my first name. Every time she reads a story about me,
that's always in front of my name."

Chris Bahr

"Gee, you've known me all these years and you still don't know how to spell my name."

> *Yogi Berra, after he received a check that said "Payable to Bearer"*

"Jose truly was the player to be named later."

> *Rocky Bridges, after Jose Gonzales changed his name to Jose Uribe*

"He's cot to help us. If he doesn't, we cot a raw deal."

> *Jim Bouton, on Cot Deal*

"My whole family likes to play basketball. George II plays for his high school team and George III and George IV and George V are going to be good players. One day we're going to have a team and call it George-town."

> *George Foreman*

"You can soon start calling me World B. Free Agent."

> *World B. Free, on his interest in becoming a free agent*

"Every time I see my name in the paper, it says Roy Green, 34. I'm starting to think my last name is 34."
Roy Green

"The only thing I don't like about him is that he named his son Orel Hershiser the fifth. My name is Durrel Norman Elvert, and I didn't name any of my kids that."
Whitey Herzog, on pitcher Orel Hershiser

"I'm a household name but not a household word."
Paul Householder

"Everywhere I looked, I saw my name—and it was spelled right."
Karl Mecklenburg, on visiting his ancestral home, Mecklenburg, Germany

"The latest is Procastin Nater."
Swen Nater, on a possible name for his child

"I like my name. Not too many people have it."

> Elvis Peacock

"Your first name's white, your second is Hispanic and your third belongs to a black. No wonder you don't know who you are."

> Mickey Rivers, on Reginald Martinez Jackson

"When I asked my dad about it, he told me that it had been a choice between that and slide."

> Golden Ruel, Kansas offensive coordinator, on how he got his first name

"I'm enjoying everything except when people put Ms. on the envelope of my letters."

> Kay Whitmore, NHL goalie

"If it's a boy, my neighbors have some friends who want me to name him Bjorn, so the headlines could read, 'BJORN ZORN BORN.'"

> Jim Zorn, on a possible name for his child

"When we lined up for the national anthem on opening day and I heard one of my players say, 'Every time we hear that song, we have a bad game.'"

Jim Leyland, on how he knew it would be a bad season for the Pirates

"Columbia was in the game right up to the national anthem."

Jim Nantz, on Columbia's 35th straight loss

"They even replay the national anthem."

Vin Scully, on the Dodgers' new scoreboard, which shows replays frequently

"I've made the national anthem a six-point underdog."

Jimmy "The Greek" Snyder, on Joe Frazier's rendition of the national anthem

"It'll be great not to have to listen to two different national anthems."

> *Mitch Webster, on being traded away*
> *from the Montreal Expos*

NERVES

"I knew this spring when the Royals asked me if I wanted to take a stress test like the players, I said 'I don't need another one—I managed Ron Davis.'"

> *Billy Gardner, on the inconsistent reliever Ron Davis*

"Lew Burdette would make coffee nervous."
> *Fred Haney*

NICKNAMES

"I can't understand why he hasn't been nicknamed Chicken. Don't you get it? 'Chicken Catcher Torre.'"

> *Bobby Bragan, on Joe Torre*

"I'd like to see Senior Miller."

Tom Brookshier, on 6'4", 235-pound
tight end Junior Miller

"We had one kid on the squad we called Spot. When a freshman beat him out for the last position, we called the new kid Spot Remover."

Benny Dees

"When I get done with Sweet Pea, he'll be Split Pea."

Greg Haugan, on fighting Pernell
"Sweet Pea" Whitaker

"I fought Sugar Ray Robinson so many times, it's a wonder I didn't get diabetes."

Jake LaMotta

"I was so ugly that when my father first saw me, he thought I had already gone ten rounds with Joe Louis."

Champ Summers, on how he got his
name

"Because they're wide awake when he hits 'em and their lights are out when he walks away."

Charlie Waters, on Aaron Mitchell,
who had the nickname "A.M./P.M."

267

"If I'd known I was gonna pitch a no-hitter today, I would have gotten a haircut."
Bo Belinsky

"If I knew he was gonna throw a no-hitter, I'd a thrown one too."
Dizzy Dean, after his brother, Paul (Daffy), threw a no-hitter

"You've got to be lucky, but if you have good stuff, it's easier to be lucky."
Sandy Koufax, on his no-hitters

NOTRE DAME

"Money is the driving force in college sports. If NBC tells Notre Dame to kick off at 3, all they ask is A.M. or P.M."
Beano Cook, on Notre Dame's $37 million contract with NBC

"Russia in the winter and Notre Dame in South Bend."

Beano Cook, on two things you never bet against

"I can't wait to get back to the restaurant and see the waiter who said, 'Cheerios and Notre Dame are different: Cheerios belong in a bowl.'"

Lou Holtz, after Notre Dame upset Florida in the 1992 Sugar Bowl

"We believe in the spirit of Notre Dame, but some people think it's false. I understand their point. If we are so blessed, then why did we go 5–6 in 1985?"

Mike Stonebreaker

"There's nothing new here. They say a lot of things trying to convince people otherwise, but the school has been looking out for Number One since time began."

Jim Walden, Iowa State football coach, on Notre Dame's decision to sign a large contract with NBC

"We had 25,000 people booing us and throwing garbage on our heads. It was like the whole country was Notre Dame."

Jerome Whitehead, on touring Brazil
while playing for Marquette

"At some schools, hope springs eternal. Here, demand springs eternal."

Larry Williams, former Notre Dame
football player

NUMBERS

"I threw about 90 percent fastballs and sliders, 50 percent fastballs, 50 percent sliders . . . wait, I'm starting to sound like Mickey Rivers."

John Butcher, on a one-hitter

"The guy in front of me got number 76 and the guy behind me got number 78."

Red Grange, on how he got his number 77

"Dave Dravecky has now thrown 66 pitches through six innings. It doesn't take a very smart guy to figure out that's 12 an inning."
> *Duane Kuiper*

"Two grand slams in a week—man, that's 7 or 8 ribbies right there."
> *Bill Madlock, on Al Oliver*

"The Sonics are 19–0 in games they've led after the fourth quarter."
> *Rich Moxley, Seattle Supersonics' PR director*

"Pitching is 80 percent of the game, the other half is hitting and fielding."
> *Mickey Rivers*

"I figured at this point in the season we'd be .500."
> *Jim Valvano, after going 5–0 at the start of the season*

"During the week I practiced law. On Sunday I *was* the law."

> *Tommy Bell, NFL referee and attorney*

"Officials are the only guys who can rob you and then get a police escort out of the stadium."

> *Ron Bolton*

"The trouble with officials is they just don't care who wins."

> *Tommy Canterbury, Centenary basketball coach*

"When we came out on the floor and I saw Louie and the three refs deciding where they were gonna eat right after the game."

> *Tom Green, basketball coach at Farleigh Dickenson, on when he knew he was in for a long night against St. John's and its coach, Lou Carnesecca*

"You can say something to popes, kings, presidents, but you can't talk to officials. In the next war, they ought to give everybody a whistle."

Abe Lemons

"You have to be respectful when arguing with an official. I usually say, 'Sir, are we watching the same game?' "

Homer Smith, former football coach at West Point

"Officiating is the only occupation in the world where the highest accolade is silence."

Earl Strom

OPTIMISM

"I was home for a week following the season before I realized we weren't in the World Series."

Bill Madlock, on the optimistic outlook of manager Chuck Tanner

"In 26 years in the pros, I haven't noticed many changes. The players are faster, bigger, smarter, and more disloyal to owners. That's about it."
George Blanda

"I've never seen so many damned idiots as the owners in sports."
Charlie Finley

"We're 28 Republicans who vote Socialist."
Art Modell, Cleveland Browns' owner, on how he and the other owners share TV money and gate receipts

"I taught Charlie all he knows about baseball. That's why I keep asking myself where I went wrong."
Hank Peters, on Charlie Finley

"The owners aren't bad. They're dumb. Marvin Miller thinks about tomorrow. They think about yesterday."
Paul Richards, on baseball owners

"If you're playing ball and thinking about managing, you're crazy. You'd be better off thinking about being an owner. It's safer."
Casey Stengel

PAIN

"Speed, strength, and the inability to register pain immediately."
Reggie Williams, on his greatest strengths as a football player

PARTY

"If music be the food of love, by all means let the band play on."
Bo Belinsky

"I didn't room with him. I roomed with his suitcase."
Ping Bodie, on Babe Ruth

"Live in it, drive it, wear it, and eat it."

Tickey Burden, on how he intended to spend the money from his first NBA contract

"Everybody who roomed with Mantle said he took five years off his career."

Whitey Ford, on Mickey Mantle

"I'll be honest: beer and women hurt a lot of us."

Rod Frawley, on why he and other Australian tennis players never lived up to expectations

"We didn't lose many games—and we never, never lost a party."

Curley Johnson, on his playing days with Joe Namath and the New York Jets

"All I know is that Richard Burton outlived James Fixx."

Sonny Jurgensen, on the virtues of a wild lifestyle

"Ninety percent I'll spend on good times, women, and Irish whiskey. The other 10 percent I'll probably waste."

> Tug McGraw

"I hope they burn all the newspapers before my kids grow up. I wouldn't want them to know what a jerk I was."

> John Montefusco

"There's nothing wrong with reading the game plan by the light of the jukebox."

> Ken Stabler

"He doesn't drink, he doesn't smoke, he doesn't chew, he doesn't stay out late, and he still can't hit .250."

> Casey Stengel, on straight-laced Bobby Richardson

"My whole life flashed before me. I couldn't believe I had been that bad."

> Lee Trevino, after being hit by lightning

"There are three things worth living for—American luxury, Japanese women, and Chinese food."
Emil Zatopek, legendary distance runner

"He was known to play night games no matter what it said on the schedule."
Vic Ziegel, on Joe Pepitone

PERSONALITY

"I don't know—I only played there nine years."
Walt Garrison, asked if Tom Landry ever smiled

"If they paid me on the basis of personality, I'd make about two dollars a year."
Mike Ivie

"You only have to bat a thousand in two things—flying and heart transplants. Everything else—you can go 4 for 5."
Beano Cook

"I'm just a caraway seed in the bakery of life."
Pete Gillen, Xavier basketball coach

"Any philosophy that can be put in a nutshell belongs there."
Branch Rickey

"Andre Dawson has a bruised knee and is listed as day-to-day. Aren't we all?"
Vin Scully

"Philosophy is just a hobby. You can't open a philosophy factory."
Dewey Selmon, on majoring in philosophy at Oklahoma

"Ryne Duren was a one-pitch pitcher. His one pitch was a wild warm-up."
> *Jim Bouton*

"Don's idea of a waste pitch is a strike."
> *Jim Brosnan, on Don Drysdale*

"Any more changes and they would have needed a new set of tires for the bullpen car."
> *Chuck Cottier, after a 13–10 Mariner win over Chicago in which 10 pitchers were used*

"My fastball, my slider, my ERA, and my blood pressure."
> *Rich Gale, on being asked what's up*

"Hell, Lou, it took 15 years to get you out of the game. Sometimes I'm out in 15 minutes."
> *Lefty Gomez, to Lou Gehrig on Gehrig's record of consecutive games played*

"Freddy Fitzsimmons is my man. He once hit me in the on-deck circle."

> Billy Herman, on the best brushback pitcher he ever saw

"He got hit so hard I had to get all the married men off the field."

> Whitey Herzog, on Ken Dayley

"After a while, I asked if I could pitch from closer in."

> Charlie Hough, after walking five batters in a row

"I'm working on a new pitch—it's called a strike."

> Jim Kern

"If it was, more pitchers would be soaking their heads instead of their arms in ice."

> Jim Longborg, on being asked if pitching was more mental than physical

"He told me to get back behind the batter, that the only thing I knew about pitching was that it was hard to hit."

> Tim McCarver, on going to the mound
> to talk to Bob Gibson about his pitch
> selection

"It's got absolutely nothing on it."

> Al Michaels, on why he calls Steve
> McCatty's new pitch the nudist

"I was in the 30-30 club at Tidewater—30 walks and 30 strikeouts."

> John Mitchell, after hearing Howard
> Johnson made the 30-30 club

"It's the best stuff I've had in a month."

> Jim Morrison, infielder, forced to
> pitch his second game in a month

"They want me to throw it over the plate, and I can't pitch that way."

> Rick Ownbey

"I may not be the bestest pitcher in the world, but I sure out-cutes 'em."

> *Satchel Paige*

"Some people throw to spots, other people throw to zones. Renie throws to continents."

> *Dan Quisenberry, on teammate Renie Martin*

"Aim the ball right at the middle of the plate, because you couldn't hit anything you aim at and maybe you will catch a corner."

> *Casey Stengel, giving advice to pitcher Tracy Stallard*

"You can't have a miracle every day—except you can when you get great pitching."

> *Casey Stengel*

"I know, Jim, but the outfielders are."

> *Jeff Torborg, taking Jim Kern out of the game even though Kern said he wasn't tired*

"He made two mistakes. The first was a slider that didn't slide. The second was a curve that didn't curve."
Richie Zisk, on Claude Osteen

PITCHING FROM THE BATTER'S PERSPECTIVE

"After watching Roger Clemens hit in the World Series, I know this is one award he'll never win."
Don Baylor, on winning the Designated Hitter Award

"For the first time in 20 years, I broke a bat the other day. Backed my car over it in the garage."
Lefty Gomez

"Even a blind dog finds a bone every once in a while."
Bruce Hurst, on his first major-league hit

"Joaquin Andujar and a curveball at the plate are complete strangers."
Tommy Lasorda

"He's such a bad hitter, sometimes someone pinch-hits for him in batting practice."
Jim Leyland, on Jeff Robinson

"You know you're pitching well when the batters look as bad as you do at the plate."
Duke Snider, on the solid pitching of Dennis Blair

PITCHING — THE CURVEBALL

━━━━━━━━━━━━━━━━━━━━

"Tom Lasorda's curveball had as much hang time as a Ray Guy punt."
Rocky Bridges

PITCHING — THE FASTBALL (OR LACK THEREOF)

━━━━━━━━━━━━━━━━━━━━

"You could catch him with a pair of pliers."
Ed Bailey, on pitcher Stu Miller's velocity

"I throw the ball harder than Nolan Ryan. It just doesn't get there as fast."

Steve Busby

"Nobody knows how fast I am. The ball doesn't get to the mitt that often."

Lefty Gomez

"Ryan is the only guy who puts fear in me. Not because he can get you out but because he can kill you."

Reggie Jackson, on Nolan Ryan

"Teams can't prepare for me in batting practice. They can't find anyone who throws as slow as I do."

Dave LaPoint

"We had him clocked at 92—45 going to Rick Dempsey and 47 going back."

Tom Lasorda, on Don Sutton's velocity

"I knew I was in trouble when they started clocking my fastball with a sundial."

Joe Magrane

"When you start to lose it, your fastball and change-up keep getting closer to one another."
Scott McGregor

"Since I don't have one, the only thing I have to fear is fear itself."
Dan Quisenberry, on how most pitchers fear losing their fastball

"I'm getting by on three pitches now—a curve, a change-up, and whatever you want to call that thing that used to be a fastball."
Frank Tanana

"He's at least half as good already—he's already throwing the ball more than 47 miles an hour."
Pete Vukovich, on comparing teammate Bob Gibson to Hall of Famer Bob Gibson

"When Duren hits you on the side, the ball doesn't come out."
Leon Wagner, on Ryne Duren

"Gibson's the luckiest pitcher I've ever seen, because he always picks the night to pitch when the other team doesn't score any runs."

Tim McCarver, on Bob Gibson

"He's unbelievable. He's like that guy in Texas who's 41—or 42 or 43."

Junior Ortiz, comparing Scott Erickson with Nolan Ryan

"Watching him pitch is like a struggling artist watching Michelangelo paint."

Jerry Reuss, on Tom Seaver

"Sometimes I hit him like I used to hit Koufax, and that's like drinking coffee with a fork. Did you ever try that?"

Willie Stargell, on Steve Carlton

"Comparing me with Sandy Koufax is like comparing Earl Scheib with Michelangelo."

Don Sutton

"My boy, I can't recall anyone loading the bases against me."

> Cy Young, when asked what his favorite pitch was with the bases loaded

PITCHING—THE KNUCKLEBALL

"It was like talking to Edison about light bulbs."

> Tom Candiotti, on discussing the knuckleball with Phil Niekro

"A stadium with the lights out."

> Charlie Hough, on ideal conditions for a knuckleball pitcher

"Watching a knuckleball pitcher is like watching Mario Andretti park a car."

> Ralph Kiner

"There are two theories on hitting the knuckleball. Unfortunately, neither one of them works."

> Charlie Lau

"It actually giggles at you as it goes by."
Rick Monday, on Phil Niekro's knuckleball

"Trying to hit him is like trying to eat Jell-O with chopsticks. Once in a while you might get a piece, but most of the time you go hungry."
Bobby Murcer, on Phil Niekro

PITCHING—RELIEF

"We developed a very scientific system for bringing in relief pitchers. We used the first one who answered the telephone."
Chuck Estrada, former pitching coach

"In 1971 I had 17 saves and got a raise. In 1985 I had 17 saves and got released."
Rollie Fingers

"Long relief is like being a plumber. Some days it's OK but when 30 septic tanks back up, it's no fun."
George Frazier

"Three more saves and he ties John the Baptist."
Hank Greenwald, *on Bruce Sutter*

"If you don't have outstanding relief pitching, you might as well piss on the fire and call in the dogs."
Whitey Herzog

"How can I intimidate batters if I look like a goddamn golf pro?"
Al Hrabosky, on being forced to shave his beard

"I was out mowing my lawn during the baseball strike. I got the front yard done and about half the back, and then I kept waiting for Goose Gossage to come out and finish it for me."
Tommy John

"Why pitch nine innings when you can get just as famous pitching two?"
Sparky Lyle

"Some people say you have to be crazy to be a reliever. Well, I don't know—I was crazy before I became one."
Sparky Lyle

"Some days you tame the tiger. And some days the tiger has you for lunch."

Tug McGraw, on relief pitching

"I'm just a garbage man. I come into a game and clean up after people's messes."

Dan Quisenberry

"When the bullpen phone rings, we just jump up and run in circles. It's like musical chairs when the music ends—whoever doesn't have a seat will go in to pitch."

Dan Quisenberry

PITCHING—
SLOW DELIVERY

"Some night Zahn's going to deliver the ball and by the time it gets there, he's going to find out that the batter has been waived."

Bob Lemon, on Geoff Zahn

"Go out there and pitch three innings or four hours, whichever comes first."

> Danny Murtaugh, to slow worker
> Steve Blass

"Some of the players have an attendance clause in their contracts. But Andy has a concession contract. Each time he pitches for us they sell more hot dogs."

> Buck Rodgers, on Andy McGaffigan's
> slow delivery

PITCHING — THE SPITBALLS

"Gaylord Perry had the only thing harder to hit than a golf ball."

> Johnny Bench

"I don't put any foreign substance on the baseball. Everything I use on it is from the good ol' USA."

> George Frazier

"Not intentionally, but I sweat easily."

> Lefty Gomez, asked if he threw a
> spitter

"He should be in the Hall of Fame with a tube of K-Y jelly attached to his plaque."

Gene Mauch, on Gaylord Perry

"He talks very well for a guy with two fingers in his mouth all the time."

Gene Mauch, on Don Drysdale

"If you tried to tackle Wyatt around the waist, you'd slide off."

Joe Pepitone, on John Wyatt's spitter

PLAYBOOKS

"Don't read Landry's playbook all the way through. Everybody dies at the end."

Peter Gent, on Tom Landry

"I haven't seen a new play since I was in high school."

Red Grange, 1974

"Last year he thought a scouting report consisted of whether we wore red or white that night."

> Bob Weiss, on how Kevin Willis's improved play was partially due to his paying more attention to scouting reports.

PLAYOFFS

"You know, if you kill somebody they sentence you to life, you serve 20 years, and you get paroled. I've never been paroled."

> Ralph Branca, on giving up Bobby Thomson's famous home run in the 1951 Giants–Dodgers playoffs

"They go on and on and on. It's like a guy telling a bad joke for 15 minutes."

> Tom Heinsohn, on the NBA playoffs

"I'm not a big fan of polls, but I'm a big fan of the Poles."

Mike Krzyzewski, on his Polish descent

POLITICS

"My family got all over me because they said Bush is only for the rich people. Then I reminded them, 'Hey, I'm rich.'"

Charles Barkley, on why he voted for President Bush

"Line them up and let them shoot jump shots from the key."

Bill Bradley, on how the Democrats should choose a presidential candidate

"Those towns in the Pacific Coast League were getting a little old. A couple of them wanted me to run for mayor."

DeWayne Buice, on his long tenure in the minors

"Any pitcher who throws at a batter and deliberately tries to hurt him is a communist."

Alvin Dark

"I'd get me a bunch of bats and balls and sneak me a couple of umpires and learn them kids behind the Iron Curtain how to take a bat and play baseball."

Dizzy Dean, on how he'd stop communism

"Whenever I play with them, I usually try to make it a foursome—the president, myself, a paramedic, and a faith healer."

Bob Hope, on playing golf with Gerald Ford

"I've never met Ollie North. I have Billy North, though."

Bill Lee

"It's like meeting Santa Claus: you go in, shake his hand, have your picture taken, and then you leave."

> Ray Mancini, after meeting President Reagan

"Most of the brothers don't make the kind of scratch I do."

> Cedric "Cornbread" Maxwell, on why he voted for conservative Jesse Helms

"I feel like Adlai Stevenson, the perennial candidate."

> Colin McLaughlin, 29-year-old pitching prospect, on self-assessment

"The Birch Society is going to expel him for making a Red famous."

> Graig Nettles, after Eric Show, a member of the John Birch Society, gave up Pete Rose's record-breaking hit

"I love it when I hear the media describe someone 44 years of age as mature and well seasoned."

> Dan Quayle, on descriptions of Nolan Ryan

"I'm a Dominican."

Jose Rijo, asked if he was a Democrat or Republican

"What was I supposed to say? Glad you got over Watergate?"

Steve Sax, after former president Nixon said that he was glad that Sax was over his throwing problems

"It's a lot tougher to be a football coach than a president. You've got four years as president, and they guard you. A coach doesn't have anyone to protect him when things go wrong."

Harry Truman

"The general takes charge as the floor leader, knows how to handle adversity and rally the troops."

Dick Vitale, on George Washington as a member of his All-Presidents basketball team

"The big guy is a space eater in the paint."

Dick Vitale, on Abraham Lincoln as a member of the same team

299

"The doctor asked me the day of the week and I said 'Friday.' Then he asked me who was the president of the United States. I said, 'Hell, I didn't know that *before* I hit my head.'"

> *Don Zimmer, on being examined after falling on his head*

POOL

"Try to hate your opponent. Even if you are playing your grandmother, try to beat her 50–0. If she already has 3, try to beat her 50–3."

> *Danny McGoorty, on why he is such a successful pool player*

"Dressing a pool player in a tuxedo is like putting whipped cream on a hotdog."

> *Minnesota Fats*

"A ballplayer's got to be kept hungry to become a big leaguer. That's why no boy from a rich family ever made the big leagues."

Joe DiMaggio

"When I was a kid in Houston, we were so poor we couldn't afford the last two letters, so we called ourselves po'."

George Foreman

"She was wrong. By the end of the season I'd sold our stereo, our car, her jewels, and our television."

Lou Holtz, on a part-time job selling cemetery plots even though his wife told him he couldn't sell anything

"The soles of my shoes were so thin I could step on a coin and tell if it was heads or tails."

Tommy Lasorda, on growing up poor

"I've got a lot of people rooting for me because there are more poor people than rich people."
Lee Trevino

"We had so little to eat that when Mom would throw a bone to the dog, he'd have to call for a fair catch."
Lee Trevino

POPULARITY

"This Thanksgiving I called all of my friends in the league. It took about 12 seconds."
Jerry Glanville

"Wherever I go people are waving at me. Maybe if I do a good job, they'll use all their fingers."
Frank King, coordinator of the 1988 Calgary Olympics

"The first time Joe said hello to some guys, he broke Earl Weaver's career record."
Jim Palmer, comparing Joe Altobelli to Earl Weaver

"What a soft job. No wonder Gehrig wouldn't take a day off for years. . . . It's like being waited on at a table. All you have to do is keep one foot on the bag."

Gabby Hartnett, Hall of Fame catcher, on playing a game at first base

"Move first base back a step."

John Lowenstein, on how to avoid close plays around first base

"I'm the best catcher in baseball other than Johnny Bench—but he's retired, I think."

Junior Ortiz, 1991

"You gotta have a catcher. If you don't have a catcher, you'll have all passed balls."

Casey Stengel, on why he picked catcher Hobie Landrith first in the expansion draft when he managed the Mets

"He's the best 23-year-old catcher I've seen since Campy—and Campy was 25 years old the first time I saw him."

Casey Stengel, on Johnny Bench

"I knew he couldn't hit, but no one told me he couldn't catch, either."

Casey Stengel, on Chris Cannizzaro

POSITIONS—FOOTBALL

"It's like saving up all your life to move out of a grubby tenement and then finding out you've moved next door."

Jim Cadile, after switching from center to guard after 11 years in the NFL

"Anything that goes up that high and travels that far ought to have a stewardess on it."

Sam Deluca, on a Ray Guy punt

"If their IQs were five points lower, they would be geraniums."

Russ Francis, on defensive linemen

304

"It's better to die at birth than jump offsides at the goal line."

Tom Freeman, offensive line coach at Arizona State

"If you're mad at your kid, you can either raise him to be a nose tackle or send him out to play on the freeway. It's about the same."

Bob Golic

"Never worry about missing a field goal. Just blame the holder and think about kicking the next one."

Lou Groza

"The way to succeed at quarterback is to call the unexpected consistently."

John Hadl

"We're the only family I know of that plays catch without facing each other."

Jay Hilgenberg, center (brother Joel is a center and their father and uncle were both centers)

"They're used to being held all the time."

Lou Holtz, on why big linemen are so secure

"He carries so many tacklers with him, he's listed in the Yellow Pages under 'Public Transportation.' "

> Bob Hope, *on running back Marcus Allen*

"This time of year, if you're breathing you're healthy."

> Kent Hull, *on offensive line play*

"I kicked six days a week and took Sunday off—just like I did last season."

> Dave Jennings, *on his training-camp routine after a lousy season the year before*

"Playing middle linebacker is like walking through a lion's cage in a three-piece pork chop suit."

> Cecil Johnson

"To me football is a contest in embarrassments. The quarterback is out there to embarrass me in front of my friends, my teammates, my coach, my wife, and my three boys. The quarterback doesn't leave me any choice. I've got to embarrass him instead."

> Alex Karras

"Playing cornerback is like being on an island—people can see you but they can't help you."
Eddie Lewis

"If Steve Young's hands are worth $40 million, I wonder how much my rear end would go for."
Trevor Matick, Steve Young's center at Brigham Young

"If you needed 4 yards, you'd give the ball to Garrison and he'd get 4 yards. If you needed 20 yards, you'd give the ball to Garrison and he'd get you 4 yards."
Don Meredith, on running back Walt Garrison

"A man who has no fear belongs in a mental institution or on special teams."
Walt Michaels

"I didn't even think kickers were eligible."
Mark Mosley, on being the Associated Press MVP after the '82 season

"Leave me alone. I'm a lineman. I want to be obscure."

> *Dennis Nelson, offensive lineman, after several members of the media followed him to his locker*

"Fritsch is so good, he practices missing."

> *Bum Phillips, on kicker Toni Fritsch*

"It's like embalming. Nobody likes it, but someone has to do it."

> *Greg Pruitt, on being a punt-return specialist*

"I think they're a bunch of slobs, but they're my kind of people."

> *John Riggins, on his opinion of the Redskins' "Hogs"*

"Each time it's like being in a head-on car accident."

> *Matt Snell, on carrying the ball in the NFL*

"Yeah—how to tackle."

> *Cliff Stoudt, on whether he learned anything after throwing three interceptions*

"You have the option of catching it by either end."

> *John Unitas, on Billy Kilmer's wobbly passes*

"I figured I was kicking against the air conditioning."

> *Bill Van Heusen, punter, after a lousy kick in the Louisiana Superdome*

"We're the only team in the history of the league that has a quarterback-coach controversy."

> *Sam Wyche, on 35-year-old Tampa Bay quarterback coach Turk Schonert's desire to play quarterback in an emergency*

"You have to know when and how to go down. The key is to have a fervent desire to be in on the next play."

> *Jim Zorn, on being a running quarterback*

"Aw, don't worry about that, Doc. If it happens, I could always come back as a forward."

> *Harold Snepsts, defenseman, advised by his doctor to wear a helmet to avoid brain damage*

PRACTICE

"The one place at Michigan State I never was late to was practice. It didn't start until I got there."

> *Duffy Daugherty, former Michigan State football coach*

"It was about normal—no worse than an ordinary death march."

> *Lou Holtz, on spring practice*

"I spent 12 years training for a career that was over in a week. Joe Namath spent one week training for a career that lasted 12 years."

> *Bruce Jenner*

"One day of practice is like one day of clean living. It doesn't do you any good."

Abe Lemons

"It's shattering when a player loses interest in camp. When you lose your desire to stand around and eat steaks, you lose everything."

John McKay

"I know my players don't like my practices, but that's OK, because I don't like their games."

Harry Neale, Vancouver Canucks' coach

"You don't get a hell of a lot of practice. It's not easy to find guys who'll come out early before games and run into you."

Mike Scioscia, on how he became a great plate blocker

"Take those fellows over to the other diamond—I want to see if they can play on the road."

Casey Stengel, on an intersquad practice

"Don't blame me. Blame the foursome ahead of me."
> *Lawrence Taylor, on why he was late for practice*

PREGNANCY

"I can still beat my husband—but I could beat him when I was nine months' pregnant."
> *Chris Evert, on playing husband Andy in tennis after her son, Alex, was born*

"That putt was so good I could feel the baby applaud."
> *Donna Horton-White, after shooting a 25-foot putt while seven months' pregnant*

"I'm not going to allow him to pick up our baby until it's at least five years old."
> *Mrs. Ed Nealy, after watching her husband drop three passes in a row*

"I just talked to the doctor. He told me her contraptions were an hour apart."

> Mackey Sasser, on his wife's pregnancy

PRISON

"I got the superstar treatment. Everybody else got bologna and water. I got bologna and milk."

> Charles Barkley, on the four hours he spent in a Milwaukee jail

"There was no place I could go to cut classes."

> Marvin Barnes, on why he earned a lot of college credit while in prison

"Three guys asked me to show them how to run out for a 250-yard pass."

> Mark Gastineau, on holding a football clinic at Rikers Island jail

"Because nobody will walk out in the middle of my speech."

> Marvin Hagler, on why he likes to
> speak at prisons

"Pete Rose, playing for his prison's softball team, deliberately gets into an argument with the umpire and gets thrown out of prison."

> David Letterman, on what he thought
> the smartest play of the year would be
> in sports

PUNS

"Show me a crazy rower who has fallen out of a one-man boating race, and I'll show you a man who is out of his scull."

> Anonymous

"I guess so; I've been fired three times."

> Dave Bristol, asked if he was a fiery
> manager

"She's become a Slav to fashion."

*Kim Cummingham, on Martina Nav-
ratilova's love of clothes*

"They had more porpoise with him in the lineup."

*Jim Enright, on why DePaul was a
better team with "Dolphin" Randolph
in the lineup*

"If Borg's parents hadn't liked the name, he might
never have been Bjorn."

Marty Indike, on Bjorn Borg

"He thinks he'll be happier in the long run."

*Frank Litsky, on Carl Lewis's switch-
ing from the 100 to the 800*

"Well, we do have a draw play."

*Pat McInally, asked how his art
classes at Harvard helped him in the
NFL*

"The first artificial fish was a plastic sturgeon."

Dr. James Nicholas, sports surgeon

"We caught them between the sand and the Sands."
> *Jerry Pettibone, Northern Illinois football coach, on playing the University of Wisconsin after playing in Hawaii and before playing in Las Vegas*

"It's a shankless job."
> *Bryan Wagner, punter, on a record 91 punts in a season*

"Jimmy Brown was the finest all-around athlete I ever saw—he was a jock of all trades."
> *Jon Weber*

REBOUNDS

"I never thought I'd lead the NBA in rebounding, but I got a lot of help from my teammates—they did a lot of missing."
> *Moses Malone*

"You know what the key to good rebounding is? Being tall."
> *Billy Packer*

RECURITING

"When I'm traveling, I ask farm boys how to get to a certain place. If they point with their fingers, I move on. If they pick up the plow and point with it, I stop and I sell them on the University of Minnesota."

Gil Dobie

"Free room and board, a new car, cash under the table, and the promise that I'd have an affair with his mother."

Jack Elway, on what it would take to have his son, John, play for him in college

"It was getting so that whenever the phone rang, I was afraid to answer. I told my parents if it was a man to tell him I wasn't home and if it was a girl that I would be right there."

Todd Krueger, highly recruited high school basketball star

"All you have to do is limit every coach to $10,000 a year—and tell him he can keep whatever he doesn't spend."

Abe Lemons, on how to reduce recruiting costs

"They say you're getting old in this profession when you go out recruiting and all the mommas look good. Right now, for me, a few of the grandmamas are starting to look pretty good."

Erk Russell, on why he was retiring at age 63 as Georgia Southern's football coach

"I like to take transfers especially from the Pac-10 because the new cars already have been paid for."

Jerry Tarkanian

"I'll watch the kids play, have a big steak with my friends, stay in a nice hotel, sign a lot of autographs, then go back to Vegas and tell my alumni how tough recruiting is."

Jerry Tarkanian, on a recruiting trip to Pittsburgh

RELATIONSHIPS

"We had a strange and wonderful relationship; he's strange and I'm wonderful."

> *Mike Ditka, on his relationship with Jim McMahon*

"When Steve and I die, we are going to be buried 60 feet, 6 inches apart."

> *Tim McCarver, on being Steve Carlton's designated catcher over the years*

"There's nothing I wouldn't do for him and there's nothing he wouldn't do for me, and that's how it's been for ten years now—we've done nothing for each other."

> *Irving Rudd, on his relationship with Tommy Hearns*

"To symbolize our great relationship, I'd like you to have this framed X ray of my ulcer."

> *Pat Williams, to 76ers' owner Harold Katz upon his resignation as general manager*

"Noah."

> *Barry Bonnel, former Seattle Mariner, asked to name his all-time favorite Mariner*

"You want to know what a real test of faith is? That's when you go to church and reach into your pocket and all you got is a $20 bill."

> *Bobby Bowden*

"God is always on the side which has the best football coach."

> *Heywood Hale Broun*

"I called up Dial-A-Prayer and they hung up on me."

> *Mack Brown, Tulane coach, after his team lost its first seven football games*

"If Jesus were on the field, he'd be pitching inside and breaking up double plays."

> *Tim Burke*

"I will not play any more tournament tennis. If I had been meant to play tennis again, God would have led me to it."

Margaret Court

"All those college football coaches who hold dressing-room prayers before a game should be forced to attend church once a week."

Duffy Daugherty

"No, that's management. I'm in sales."

Reverend John Durkin, asked if he were responsible for perfect weather at a golf tournament

"More than being concerned with who's going to win the Super Bowl, I feel the Lord is probably more concerned that they might find a day other than Sunday to play it on."

Billy Graham

"If the 11th Commandment was 'Thou shalt not covet thy neighbor's players,' I'd be on my way to hell, big-time."

Rick Majerus, on stealing players for Utah who would have played for Brigham Young

"I believe if God had ever managed, he would have been very aggressive—the way I manage."

> *Billy Martin*

"You do a lot of praying, but most of the time the answer is no."

> *John McKay, on why coaching an expansion team is like a religious experience*

"I'd have two wives. You can get away with that out there."

> *Robert Parish, on his reaction to rumors he was going to be traded to the Utah Jazz*

"If Jesus were a football player, he'd play fair, he'd play clean, and he'd put the guy across the line on his butt."

> *Barry Rice, Liberty University football player*

"I've found that prayers work best when you have big players."

> *Knute Rockne*

"I'm not Catholic."

> John Salley, on why he converted the
> former house of the Detroit arch-
> bishop into a bachelor pad for himself

"I don't know. What's his number?"

> Billy Tubbs, asked if he thought God
> was on the opponent's side after an
> Oklahoma loss

"The good father did a great job for us. When we fell
65 points behind, he started administering last rites."

> Jim Valvano, on having a priest on the
> bench during a game against Syracuse
> when Valvano coached at Bucknell

REPUTATION

"He's got a great reputation, but nobody knows anything about him."

> Ray Malavasi, on June Jones III .

"His reputation preceded him before he got here."

> Don Mattingly, on Dwight Gooden

"Look, why don't we talk about this Monday when you pick up my trash."

Sean Farrell, Tampa Bay Buccaneers guard, to a heckling fan

"The only game ball I ever got in Chicago I stole."

Charlie Ford, former Chicago Bears cornerback

"I kept hearing the Braves were trying to bring Atlanta its first-ever pro sports championship. I guess some people have short memories."

Martina Navratilova, on the Atlanta Thunder, which won the World Team Tennis championship

"Whenever I decided to release a player, I always had his room searched for a gun. You couldn't take many chances with some of these birds."

Casey Stengel

"I remember one time I'm batting against the Dodgers in Milwaukee. They lead 2–1, it's the bottom of the ninth, bases loaded for us, two outs, and the pitcher has a full count on me. I look over to the Dodgers' dugout, and they're all in street clothes."

Bob Uecker

"They broke it to me gently. The manager came up to me before a game and told me they didn't allow visitors in the clubhouse."

Bob Uecker, on being cut by a ball club

RESTAURANTS

"I'll tell you what: if I pulled up in front of a restaurant and he came out to park my car, I'd eat somewhere else."

Bob Brenly, on Juan Berenguer

"Today the biggest decisions I make aren't related to the heavyweight title. They are whether I visit McDonald's, Burger King, Wendy's, or Jack-in-the-Box."

George Foreman, on his priorities as a boxer

"If Al were dining alone, he'd still use his butter knife."

> *Steve Garvey, on the gentlemanly qualities of Al Downing*

"This has been a very peculiar year. I've seen and done a lot of things that I didn't think were possible, like ... a multimillion-dollar athlete like Dan Quisenberry eating at Burger King."

> *Joe Magrane*

"If the waitress has dirty ankles, the chili should be good."

> *Al McGuire*

"I've seen him order everything on the menu except 'Thank you for dining with us.'"

> *Jerry Royster, on Dale Murphy*

"He thinks a balanced meal is a Big Mac in each hand."

> *Pat Williams, on heavyset Stanley Roberts*

RETIREMENT

"Most people retire to play golf and fish. I do that now."

> *Julius Boros, professional golfer, explaining why he didn't retire after the age of 55*

"The thing that really sealed it was getting chosen to play in an old-timers' game and I hadn't even retired yet."

> *Ruben Carter, defensive lineman*

"I'm not a boxer. I'm only going to do this once."

> *Randy Cross, on retiring from football*

"I don't want to be in your future. It's frustrating enough being in your present."

> *Roger Erickson, retiring from baseball after the Yankees demoted him to Columbus*

"I had the bases full, a full count, and the game on the line—and I was thinking of my next alimony payment."

> Bob Gibson, on when he knew it was time to retire

"As I walked back to the dugout after striking out, I looked into the stands and saw my wife and kids booing me."

> Fran Healy, on why he decided to retire

"Ted Williams and I have a lot in common. We both hit home runs in our last major-league at-bats. The only difference was he knew it was his last. I was released the next day."

> Richie Hebner

"I knew it was time to retire when I was driving down the lane and got called for a three-second violation."

> Johnny Kerr

"I eat less, weigh less, train less, and care less."

> Ray Mancini, after retiring from boxing

"In one day, I went from a negative presence to a man with a great past."

Jim Palmer, after he retired

"I ain't doing a damn thing, and I don't start until noon."

Bum Phillips, on what he does during retirement

"When a man retires, his wife gets twice the husband but only half the income."

Chi Chi Rodriguez

"I'm doing what every retired Floridian does: Play golf. Watch the sunset. Wait for the mailman. And drive slowly."

Joe Sambito

"I've always done what was best for the club. Like this week, when I retired."

Kent Tekulve

"I married him for better or worse, but not for lunch."
Mrs. George Weiss, after her husband retired as Yankees' general manager

"Somebody will have to come out and take the uniform off me, and the guy who comes after it had better bring help."
Early Wynn

RIFLERY

"Contrary to popular belief, we do not put the two teams at opposite ends of the range."
Tom Jones, VMI athletic director, on riflery

RIVALRIES

"All literary men are Red Sox fans—to be a Yankees fan in a literate society is to endanger your life."
John Cheever

"The battery at Yankee Stadium last night was Louis pitching, Schmeling catching."

> *Bob Considine, after Joe Louis demolished Max Schmeling in their rematch for the heavyweight title*

"Buddy doesn't have many rules, but one of them is don't lose to the Cowboys."

> *Mike Golic, on former Philadelphia Eagles' coach Buddy Ryan*

"Do the Yankees like the Red Sox?"

> *Gary Kasparov, asked if he liked his chess rival Anatoly Karpov*

RODEO

"We don't even get the quality clowns."

> *Lynn Jonkowski, on the difference between men's and women's rodeo*

"Rodeoing is about the only sport you can't fix. You'd have to talk to the bulls and horses, and they wouldn't understand you."

Bill Lunderman

ROOKIES

"When I first signed with the Yankees, the regulars wouldn't talk to you until you were with the team three or four years. Nowadays, the rookies get $100,000 to sign and they don't talk to the regulars."

Lefty Gomez

"If I had done everything I was supposed to up to now, I'd be leading in homers, have the highest batting average, have given $1,000 to the cancer fund, and be married to Marie Osmond."

Clint Hurdle, on his expectations as a rookie

"How can you haze rookies when they all make more money than you do?"

Kiki Vandeweghe

"Yeah, but they all talk to each other."

> Brady Anderson, on being told that
> Queen Elizabeth, whom he and his
> Orioles teammates had just met, and
> Princess Caroline weren't related

"Nice to meet you, King."

> Yogi Berra, on meeting King George V

"So I could become someone who could shake the king's hand."

> Brahim Boutayeb, Olympic 10,000-
> meter gold medalist from Morocco,
> asked why he wanted to become a
> runner

"The only thing I've noticed is that when I come into the locker room they all bow."

> Martina Navratilova, asked if her ri-
> vals were intimidated by her

RULES

"I believe in rules. Sure I do. If there weren't any rules, how could you break them?"
Leo Durocher

RUNNING

"Running is an unnatural act, except from enemies and to the bathroom."
Anonymous

"The only reason I would take up jogging is so that I could hear heavy breathing again."
Erma Bombeck

"I hope I haven't missed dinner. I'm starved."
Charles Hardy, last finisher in the 1981 Boston Marathon, with a time of 6 hours, 38 minutes

"Hell no. If I die, I want to be sick."
Abe Lemons, asked if he wanted to take up running

"I finished 837 in a field of 837, with a medical van and a motorcycle cop on my tail all the way. It made me feel like George Bush."

> *Rick Majerus, after losing 100 pounds and running in his first marathon*

"Because I'm good at it."

> *Frank Shorter, asked why he runs marathons*

SCHEDULES

"There are a lot of guys who played tough schedules who are working at K-mart."

> *George Raveling, on playing a lot of home games when he coached at Iowa*

"There are more games in the second half than the first."

> *Mickey Rivers, on why he was opposed to an early-season players' strike*

SCHOOL

"I didn't do so hot in the first grade either."
Dizzy Dean, on why he quit school after second grade

"It didn't bother me that I ranked 234th in my high school graduating class of 273—until I heard the principal say that it was a stupid class."
Lou Holtz

"When I get through managing, I'm going to open up a kindergarten."
Billy Martin

SCORING

"Much ado about nothing to nothing."
Tim Cohane, after Pittsburgh's third straight scoreless tie against Fordham in 1937

"The game plan was for me to score the first 212, but I got tired."

> *Kevin McHale, after scoring 11 points in the first two and a half minutes of a game*

SEASON

"It's not the winters that bother me. It's the summers."

> *Walt Alston, asked if he had a pleasant winter*

"In Boston, as I recall."

> *Bobby Mattick, newly named manager of the Toronto Blue Jays, who were 53–109 the previous season, asked where he thought the team would finish*

"Yes, that's correct—20,000 different ladies. At my age that equals about having sex with 1.2 women a day every day since I was 15."

Wilt Chamberlain, on claims he slept with 20,000 women

"That was a complicated play, folks. So let's have a replay for all you fans scoring in bed."

Bob Kelly, hockey announcer

"I don't talk to people when I'm naked—especially women, unless they're on top of me or I'm on top of them."

Jack Morris, on allowing women in the locker room

"I love football. I really love football. As far as I'm concerned, it's the second best thing in the world."

Joe Namath

"Going to bed with a woman the night before a game never hurt a ballplayer. It's staying up all night looking for one that does him in."
Casey Stengel

SHOOTING

"Sometimes we have to remind Demetrius you don't get any extra points for degrees of difficulty."
Roy Chipman, on Demetrius Gore

"As long as it's indoors, it's a good shot."
Benny Dees, explaining the shooting philosophy of Robyn Davis

"I like to take all the shots in a tough situation. As a matter of fact, I like to take all the shots."
Mike Mitchell, after hitting some clutch shots in a game

"When I step into the building, you've got to get me the ball. When I step off the bus, I'm open."
Chuck Person, on his shot selection

"Coach Musselman wanted me to run the offense, play defense, call switches, and pass the ball. I was ready to do it all—but pass the ball? Never!"
David Rivers

"This year we plan to run and shoot. Next season we hope to run and score."
Billy Tubbs

SHOPPING

"He plays baseball like my wife shops—all day long."
Tommy Lasorda, on Steve Sax

SKIING

"Skiing is the only sport where you spend an arm and a leg to break an arm and a leg."
Anonymous

"I do not participate in any sport with ambulances at the bottom of the hill."

       Erma Bombeck

"We skiers know that falling down isn't important; it's getting up again."

       Gerald Ford

"Talking from morning to night about sex has helped my skiing, because I talk about movement, about looking good, about taking risks."

       Dr. Ruth Westheimer

SLEEP

"The only thing he fears is sleep."

       Jimmy Dykes, on Don Larsen

"I think sleeping was my problem in school. If school had started at four o'clock in the afternoon, I'd be a college graduate today."

       George Foreman

"With me, Johnny Carson is only a rumor."

Roger Laurin, racing trainer, on being an early sleeper

"Like a baby—for two and half hours."

Bum Phillips, on how he slept after a loss

"I overslept."

Claudell Washington, explaining why it took him four days to show up after being traded by Texas to the White Sox

SLUMPS

"Slumps are like a soft bed. They're easy to get into and hard to get out of."

Johnny Bench

"Slump? I ain't in no slump. I just ain't hitting."

Yogi Berra

"When you're going like this, it looks like even the umpires have gloves."

> Pete Rose, going through a rare slump

"We are in such a slump that even the ones that are drinkin' aren't hittin'."

> Casey Stengel

"We gotta trade him while he's still hot."

> Casey Stengel, on Don Zimmer's getting two hits in a row after going through an 0 for 34 slump

"I have an Alka-Seltzer bat. You know—plop, plop, fizz, fizz. When the pitchers see me walking up there they say, 'Oh, what a relief it is.' "

> Andy Van Slyke

"Take your bat with you."

> Earl Weaver, when told that slumping Al Bumbry was going to a chapel service

"I live so far out in the country that I have to walk toward town to go hunting."

Rocky Bridges

"It was the day one guy died and I was playing a game out of town."

John Campbell, on how his hometown of Blenheim, South Carolina, lost a quarter of its population in a 24-hour period

"It's a very small town. It's so small, in fact, that the number-one industry there is taking bottles back to the store."

Monte Clark, on his hometown of Kingsburg, California

"I grew up in a town that was so mean, hitchhikers would go the other way."

Ellis Clary

"Bristol was so small that the Howard Johnson's only served vanilla."

> Billy Gardner, on playing in the minors for a town near the Tennessee-Virginia state line

"It's so small we don't even have a town drunk. Everyone has to take a turn."

> Stan Hack, on his hometown of Grand Detour, Illinois

"The telephone directory has only one yellow page."

> Toby Harrah, on his small hometown

"Absolutely. There are a thousand better coaches in the cities, but I'm the best in the country."

> Lou Holtz, on whether he agrees with those who call him the best coach in the country

"It was the first time I met anyone that I hadn't met before."

> John Kruk, on the first time he went beyond his hometown of Keyser, West Virginia

"Living in a small town in Texas ain't half bad—if you own it."

Bobby Layne, on Lubbock, Texas

"Not much goes in or out of there, except Charles Kuralt a couple of times a year."

Joe Magrane, on his hometown of Moreland, Kentucky

"I want to be a surfer. . . . I spent my first minor-league season at Waterloo, Iowa. When I was assigned there, I thought, 'Great—Waterloo. It has to be near an ocean.' "

Greg Minton

"It was so small we didn't have a village idiot. My brother and I had to take turns."

Dick Motta, on his hometown of Union, Utah

"The gourmet shop's cheese of the week is Velveeta. The all-night diner closes at 4:30 in the afternoon."

Lou Piniella, on Plant City, Florida, the Reds' spring-training home

"I was really glad to see Italy win. All of the guys on the team were Italian."

> Tom Lasorda, on Italy's winning the World Cup

"First love, second football. Maybe photo finish."

> Giamperiero Masieri, soccer star, on the importance of soccer in Italy

"Five years. That's how long it takes for naturalization, isn't it?"

> Rinus Michaels, former U.S. soccer coach, asked how long it would take an American citizen to be a soccer star

"Some people think football is a matter of life and death. I can assure you it is much more serious than that."

> Bill Shankly, on the importance of soccer in Europe

"I'm a rock star because I couldn't be a soccer star."
Rod Stewart

SOCIAL LIFE

"If we didn't have a huddle, Jim would have no social life."
Phil Simms, on Jim Burt

"I've got a friend who is a nun, and she has a better social life than I have."
Wendy Turnbull, on her social life as a tennis player

SPACE

"That guy's the best walk-on since Neil Armstrong."
Gordon Chiesa, after walk-on Ralph Lewis scored 31 points and had 18 rebounds for Manhattan

"When Neil Armstrong set foot on the moon, he found a baseball that Jimmy Foxx hit off me in 1937."
Lefty Gomez

"Well, I'll tell you, young fella, to be truthful and honest and perfectly frank about it, I'm 83 years old, which ain't bad. To be truthful and honest and frank about it, the thing I'd like to be right now is an astronaut."
Casey Stengel

"I don't know why NASA spends all that money on the space shuttle. All they've got to do is give Manute some tools and let him reach up and fix things."
Mychal Thompson, on 7'6" Manute Bol

SPEED

"I'm so fast I could hit you before God gets the news."
Muhammad Ali

"He can run anytime he wants. I'm giving him the red light."

Yogi Berra, on Rickey Henderson

"I haven't hit him yet, and now I never will."

Doug Buffone, on hearing that the great scrambler Fran Tarkenton was retiring

"She plays tennis like she's double-parked."

Mary Carillo, on Andrea Jaeger's impatient style of play

"The kid is slower than erosion."

Gordon Chiesa, on former Manhattan player Tim Cain

"Cool Papa Bell was so fast he could get out of bed, turn out the lights across the room, and be back in bed under the covers before the lights went out."

Josh Gibson

"Maybe I have lost a step, but I had a few to lose."

Roy Green, wide receiver, on turning 34

"He must shower in Vaseline."

Lester Hayes, on Randall Cunningham

"I knew he was fast, but I never knew how fast until I saw him playing tennis by himself."

Lou Holtz, on Rocket Ismail

"When I started out I looked like Barry Sanders, and when I finished I looked like Colonel Sanders."

Reggie Johnson, 250-pound tight end, on running back a kick 34 yards

"I kind of like Craig Morton. I think he's an overachiever. The main reason I like him, though, is because he can't run out of the pocket."

Jack Lambert

"Bruce Benedict is so slow he'd finish third in a race with a pregnant woman."

Tommy Lasorda

"I like to spread them out. That way I don't get tired."

Mike LaValliere, on his first triple in his last 1,346 at-bats

351

"He looked like a pearl in Prell."

*Jim Leyland, describing John Smiley
running from first to third on a single*

"I thought they'd stop the game and give me second base."

*Milt May, on stealing a base for the
first time in five years*

"One time he hit a line drive right past my ear. I turned around and saw the ball hit his ass sliding into second base."

Satchel Paige, on Cool Papa Bell

"It's like trying to keep water from going over the dam. You know what's coming, but you're powerless."

Harry Parker, on Lou Brock

"The only way you can do that is by breaking into the equipment room."

*Pete Rose, on Greg Luzinski's claims
that he would steal 20 bases in 1981*

"That's one rush Jim Plunkett could avoid."
> *Garry Shandling, on lava from a volcano in Hawaii traveling three feet an hour*

"The only running I do is from sideline to huddle and from huddle to sideline. Anything beyond that would get us penalized for delay of game."
> *Norm Snead*

"His only limitation is his ability to move around."
> *Joe Torre, on Pedro Guerrero's mobility*

"Rich Dauer is so slow that we time him from home to first with a calendar."
> *Earl Weaver*

"He has two speeds—here he comes and there he goes."
> *Barry Wilburn, on Roy Green*

"You have to learn how not to get a jump on the ball."
> *Earl Williams, on going seven seasons without a stolen base*

"Do you mean the bird or stealin'?"

> *Frank Layden, quoting the response of a draft choice when Layden tested his intelligence by asking him how to spell* robin

"It took me five years to learn how to spell Chattanooga and then I had to move to Albuquerque."

> *Joe Morrison, college football coach, on moving from Tennessee-Chattanooga to New Mexico*

"I asked him to spell Mississippi. He said, 'The state or the river?' "

> *George Raveling, on testing the intelligence of a recruit*

SPORTS

"Generally speaking, I look upon sports as dangerous and tiring activities performed by people with whom I share nothing except the right to trial by jury."

> *Fran Lebowitz*

"The Winter Olympics are easier. Nobody asks whether any of the bobsledders are going to arbitration."

> Tim McCarver, on the difference between baseball announcing and hosting the Winter Olympics

"Oh, wrestling is much tougher. Every night you have to drive a lot of miles to another arena."

> Leo Nomellini, comparing professional wrestling and professional football

"I hate all sports as rabidly as a person who likes sports hates common sense."

> H. L. Mencken

"Sports is the only profession I know that when you retire, you have to go to work."

> Earl Monroe

"Sports is the only entertainment where, no matter how many times you go back, you never know the ending."

> Neil Simon

"I always turn to the sports section first. The sports section records people's accomplishments; the front page, nothing but men's failures."

Earl Warren

SPORTS COMPARISONS

"If I was going to get beat up, I wanted to be indoors where it was warm."

Tom Heinsohn, on why he picked basketball over football at Holy Cross

"After the season with the Celtics, he said he wouldn't pitch for the Red Sox for four weeks because it took him that long to get out of shape."

Bill Russell, on professional baseball and basketball player Gene Conley

"We'd have thirty seconds of respectful silence and then continue with enthusiasm."

> *George Atkinson, on the reaction of players and coaches if the press box blew up*

"The Lord taught me to love everybody, but the last ones I learned to love were the sportswriters."
Alvin Dark

"What's the difference between a three-week-old puppy and a sportswriter? In six weeks, the puppy stops whining."
Mike Ditka

"Reggie once said that the only people he can relate to are the writers. That's because they are the only ones who benefit from hearing his crap."

> *Sparky Lyle, on Reggie Jackson*

"I always thought that to win a Pulitzer you had to bring down a government, not just quote Tommy Lasorda correctly."

Jim Murray, on winning a Pulitzer Prize

"The best three years of their lives are spent in the third grade."

George Raveling, on sportswriters

"Sportswriting is just like driving a taxi. It ain't the work you enjoy, it's the people you run into."

Blackie Sherrod

"I think it's funny that almost all the sportswriters who are always asking why Craig doesn't lose weight are heavier than he is."

Mrs. Craig Stadler, on her heavyset golfer husband

"It was a brain transplant. I got a sportswriter's brain so I could be sure I had one that hadn't been used."

Norm Van Brocklin, on his 1980 brain surgery

"In this ballpark, I feel when you walk to the plate you're in scoring position."

Don Baylor, on the Seattle Kingdome

"It gets late early out there."

Yogi Berra, on the shadows in Yankee Stadium

"They'd be doing everyone a favor if they bombed this place."

Bill Buckner, on Candlestick Park

"I don't know. I've never pitched in a phone booth before."

Gene Conley, asked how he would like pitching at Fenway Park

"The damned thing is so close I scrape my knuckles on it every time I throw a sidearm curve."

Bob Feller, on the Green Monster, Fenway Park's famed left-field wall

"That's a high chopper over the mound."

> *Dave Gallagher, on a helicopter over Tiger Stadium*

"I have a large glove and it's very loose. The wind swirls out there and it closed my glove."

> *Larry Herndon, explaining how he missed a fly ball in a game at Candlestick Park*

"Sitting in the dugout at Candlestick is like being at the bottom of a toilet. All the tissues come in and nobody flushes."

> *Whitey Herzog*

"Well, all I can say is that the old neighborhood was so tough they raffled off two police cars with the cops in them."

> *Frank Lucchesi, on the neighborhood around Connie Mack Stadium*

"I'll be prepared for it. Our seventh-grade trip was to Antarctica. Maybe I'll take a Bunsen burner over there, maybe take some powdered food. For lack of a better word, by the end of the game, I'd like to say that I breezed through nine innings."

> *Joe Magrane, anticipating his first game at Candlestick Park*

"Candlestick was built on the water. It should have been built under it."

Roger Maris

"If this is a ballpark, I'm a Chinese aviator."

Billy Martin, on the Metrodome

"I love to play in Madison Square Garden. I don't care if it was in the Sahara Desert. Just the name is legend."

George McGinnis

"I'm against anyone dropping atom bombs, except for on the Metrodome."

Dan Quisenberry

"This wouldn't be such a bad place to play if it wasn't for that wind. I guess that's like saying hell wouldn't be such a bad place if it wasn't so hot."

Jerry Reuss, on Candlestick Park

"It was the coldest gym I ever played in. A couple of rebounds came down with frost on them."

Brook Steppe, former Pistons guard, on the Pontiac Silverdome

361

"New York will be happy to share the Giants with our great sister state. Let them be the New York Giants when they win and the New Jersey Giants when they lose."

>   *Mario Cuomo, on the New York Giants playing in New Jersey*

"You're not legally dead until you lose your tan."

>   *Tommy Lasorda, on California*

"I won't say it's remote up here, but my last speech was reviewed in *Field and Stream*."

>   *George Raveling, on coaching at Washington State*

"There were other cities besides the Garden State who wanted the Yankees."

>   *Phil Rizzuto, on New Jersey*

"My earned run average is so high it looks like an AM radio station."

> *Jim Gott, on a few bad outings in spring training*

"I think I've got a great shot at 20 wins—I mean, I'm 19–23 now, so I've only got one to go."

> *Dave Heaverlo, on his career record*

"Statistics are like loose women: once you get them, you can do anything you want with them."

> *Walt Michaels*

"Statistics are like bikinis: they show a lot but not everything."

> *Lou Piniella*

"Statistics are used like a drunk uses a lamp post—for support, not illumination."

> *Vin Scully*

"Statistics say he was the second-best second baseman in the league, but that doesn't count the balls he couldn't get to."

> Dick Williams, on Padres second baseman Juan Bonilla

GEORGE STEINBRENNER

"Steinbrenner fired the horse and then had Billy Martin run in the Preakness."

> Chris Berman, after Steinbrenner's Kentucky Derby horse, Eternal Prince, finished 12th

"It was a beautiful thing to behold, with all 36 oars working in unison."

> Jack Buck, on Steinbrenner's yacht

"A nervous breakdown with a big weekly paycheck."

> Bucky Dent, on working for Steinbrenner

"The more we lose, the more Steinbrenner will fly. And the more he flies, the better the chance there will be a plane crash."

Dock Ellis

"As soon as I get there, I'm going to rip Steinbrenner just to get it out of the way."

Mickey Hatcher, on rumors he was going to be traded to the Yankees

"I wanted to find out if the diamond was real, so I cut the glass on my coffee table with it. Then I found out the coffee table was worth more than the ring."

Sparky Lyle, on the diamond rings Steinbrenner gave the Yankees after winning the World Series

"Nothing is more limited than being a limited partner of George's."

John McMullen

"It's a good thing Babe Ruth isn't still here. If he was, George would have him bat seventh and tell him he's overweight."

Graig Nettles

"How do you know when George Steinbrenner is lying? When you see his lips move."

Jerry Reinsdorf

"Every time you go into his office he greets you warmly and shakes you by the throat."

Al Rosen, on working for Stein-
brenner

"We plan absent ownership. I'll stick to building ships."

George Steinbrenner, 1973

"My heel felt just like George Steinbrenner: irritating, painful, nagging, and wouldn't go away."

Mychal Thompson

STUPIDITY

"You have to be stupid, and this works out well for me. I am very immature, and I work at it every day of my life."

Bubba Baker, on what it takes to play
in the NFL

"Well, Rolf, do you want to kick with the wind or against it?"

Don Coryell, to kicker Rolf Benirschke before a game in the Seattle Kingdome

"There's no way they can bury 12 people out there."

Bob Kearney, on the 12 monuments in centerfield at Yankee Stadium

"You could tell five guys to go over to the post office at two o'clock and one of them wouldn't be there. So why have so many tricky plays?"

Abe Lemons

"I couldn't resist—I had such a great jump on the pitcher."

Lou Novikoff, on stealing third with the bases loaded

"He's like the planet Jupiter. We know he's out there, but we're not sure what he's doing."

Pierre Page, on Quebec Nordiques defenseman Bryan Fogarty

"Tell a ballplayer something a thousand times—then tell him again, because that might be the time he'll understand something."

Paul Richards

"I want to gain 1,500 or 2,000 yards, whichever comes first."

George Rogers, on his goal for the season

"He is the first player to make the major leagues on one brain cell."

Roy Smalley, on Mickey Hatcher

"Are you any relation to your brother Marv?"

Leon Wood, introducing himself to TV announcer Steve Albert

SUPERSTITIONS

"None, really. But I never pitch well on days they play the national anthem."

Mike Flanagan, asked if he had any superstitions

368

"We took his glove to the chapel this morning. We got the devil out of it."

> *Terry Puhl, referring to Enos Cabell's four errors in eight games*

"I had only one superstition. I made sure to touch all the bases when I hit a home run."

> *Babe Ruth*

"One, don't call somebody a bad name if they're holding a loaded pistol. Two, don't call your girlfriend Tina if her name is Vivian."

> *George Underwood, East Tennessee State basketball player, on any superstitions he might have*

"Only calling Nancy Reagan."

> *Andy Van Slyke, asked if he had any pregame superstitions after finding out that the former First Lady consulted an astrologist*

"His voice could peel the skin off a potato, and when he's on one of his shriek rolls, he breaks only for commercials and small animals."

Norman Chad, on Dick Vitale

"I've discovered that the less I say, the more rumors I start."

Bobby Clarke

"It was cheese, salami, and tongue. You had to figure with Carter, it was mostly tongue. There was no way I could bring myself to eat that."

Mark Davis, on a Gary Carter sandwich at the Stage Deli

"You can plant two thousand rows of corn with the fertilizer Lasorda spreads around."

Joe Garagiola, on Tom Lasorda

"Having dinner with Tommy Lasorda is like pitching a game in the big leagues. Afterwards, you need three days' rest."

Joe Garagiola

"One day Don King will asphyxiate by the force of his own exhaust."

Carmen Graciano

"I love to listen to Bo talk. Maybe it's because I don't have much choice when we're together."

Lou Holtz, on Bo Schembechler

"The best way to save face is by keeping the lower part of it shut."

Lou Holtz

"I talked to him briefly on the phone for an hour and a half."

Tony Kornheiser, on Joe Theismann

"Ask him for the time and he'll tell you how to make a watch."

Bob Lemon, on Tommy John

"If talking was an Olympic sport, Theismann is Jim Thorpe."

Mike Lupica, on Joe Theismann

"My broadcast partners are Joe Theismann and Dick Vitale, so I am unaccustomed to public speaking."

Mike Patrick

"If I wasn't talking, I wouldn't know what to say."

Glenn "Chico" Resch

"Every once in a while he has to come up for a breath."

Milt Richman, on Sparky Anderson

"He never shuts up. The way to test a Timex watch would be to strap it to Weaver's tongue."

Marty Springstead, on Earl Weaver

"I know that if he shot off his mouth long enough, he'd get something right."

*Billy Tubbs, referring to Dick Vitale,
who called Tubbs an offensive genius*

"Dark threw stools; Hutch threw rooms."

> Ed Bailey, on contrasting the tantrums of Al Dark and Fred Hutchinson

"When we followed Detroit into a city, we could always tell how Hutch fared. If we got stools in the dressing room, we knew he had won. If we got kindling, we knew he had lost."

> Yogi Berra, on Fred Hutchinson

"They throw their clubs backwards and that's wrong. You should always throw a club ahead of you so that you don't have to walk any extra distance to get it."

> Tommy Bolt, advising young golfers on how best to throw tantrums

"It was interesting playing tennis with Mike—at least as long as his racquet lasted."

> Tom Landry, on Mike Ditka's temper

"You buy a couch and he throws in a chair."

Digger Phelps, imagining chair-and-tantrum-thrower Bobby Knight as the owner of a furniture business

"My arm has felt so bad since I retired that I can't even throw a tantrum."

Steve Stone

"He was a moody guy, a tantrum thrower like me, but when he punched a locker or something he always did it with his right hand. He was a careful tantrum thrower."

Ted Williams, on Lefty Grove

TAXES

"The government should legalize it—then tax it out of business."

Joey Adams, on how to end sports gambling

"I was thinking I was going to be a rich man until the government stepped in and took it all."

> Luc Longley, figuring he was going to reap the benefits of a huge contract

"Is that before or after taxes?"

> Sam Perkins, after signing a $19 million contract with the Lakers

"He wants to vote and cheat on his taxes like everyone else."

> Mychal Thompson, on Yugoslavian teammate Vlade Divac

TEAMS—BASEBALL

"You have to have a certain dullness of mind and spirit to play here. I went through psychoanalysis, and that helped me deal with my Cubness."

> Jim Brosnan, on the Cubs

"What does a mama bear on the pill have in common with the World Series? No cubs."

Harry Caray, on the Cubs

"I'd rather play in hell than for the Angels."

Alex Johnson

"It was like having your mother throw you out of the house on Christmas Eve."

Ed Lynch, on being traded from the Mets to the Cubs

"He spent eight years in the big leagues, plus four years with the Pirates."

Don Mattingly, on Rick Rhoden

"When I was a kid, I wanted to play baseball and join the circus. With the Yankees, I've been able to do both."

Graig Nettles

"Tradition here in St. Louis is Stan Musial coming into the clubhouse and making the rounds. Tradition in San Diego is Nate Colbert coming into the clubhouse and trying to sell you a used car."

Bob Shirley, on the Padres

"They're a shelter all right. A bomb shelter."
*Ted Turner, asked if a lousy Braves
team was a good tax shelter*

"With the Cardinals I'd come in and find everyone reading the stock market reports. With the Pirates, I come in and find everyone checking the papers to see if Hulk Hogan won."
Andy Van Slyke

"Rooting for the Yankees is like rooting for U.S. Steel."
Bill Veeck

"I owe the Pirates some loyalty because they opened the gates of hell and got me out of Seattle."
Glenn Wilson

"The only chance you've got around here is to be dead, retired, or Reggie."
Dave Winfield, on the Yankees

377

"They don't buy all those banners at Woolworth's."

Kareem Abdul-Jabbar, on the great Celtics tradition

"The Lakers are so good they could run a fast break with a medicine ball."

Rich Donnelly

"I call Los Angeles the city of alternatives. If you don't like mountains, we got the ocean. If you don't like Knott's Berry Farm, we've got Disneyland. If you don't like basketball, we've got the Clippers."

Arsenio Hall

"For a bunch of guys who would rather pass kidney stones than a basketball, it was pretty amazing."

Bob Weiss, on the often-selfish Atlanta Hawks playing good team ball

TEETH

"Kingman was like a cavity that made your whole mouth sore."

Bill Caudill, on Dave Kingman

"Can anyone tell me where I can get some dental floss that's six inches wide?"

Leon Spinks

TELEVISION

"If we ever get a divorce, the only way he'd know about it was if they announced it on the 'Wide World of Sports.'"

Dr. Joyce Brothers, on her husband's addiction to sports on TV

"His thinking is so fouled up that it takes him an hour and a half to watch '60 Minutes.'"

Kirk Gibson, on Dave Rozema

"Lem's sort of like an Andy Griffith character. You know—take it easy, don't panic, we'll think of something. You need an Andy Griffith on this team. We've got a lot of guys like Don Knotts."

Jay Johnstone, on former Yankees' manager Bob Lemon

"While Kevin McHale was shooting free throws, I could hear him on the bench saying 'Miss—c'mon, Herman Munster, miss.' Anybody with a sense of humor like that gets my vote."

Cedric Maxwell, on why he would vote for Cory Blackwell of the SuperSonics as the rookie of the year

"What would I do that for? It only gets Spanish stations."

Jeff Stone, after playing winter ball in Venezuela and being asked why he wouldn't take his TV back to the U.S.

TENNIS

"The serve was invented so that the net can play."
Bill Cosby

"In baseball you have to leave your sensitivity at the door. If you can't take it, play tennis."

> Ron Darling, on the sensitivity of former teammate Gregg Jefferies

"My teenage daughter has a new boyfriend. My son just made the basketball team in junior high school. And my wife found a tennis partner she can beat."

> Lou Holtz, on why he was reluctant to leave New York

"Unless there's some emotional tie, I'd rather play tennis."

> Bianca Jagger, on sex

"A perfect combination of violent action taking place in an atmosphere of total tranquility."

> Billie Jean King

"If you see a tennis player who looks as if he is working very hard, then that means he isn't very good."

> Helen Wills Moody

"She was beside herself—which, come to think of it,
would make a great doubles team."

> Scott Ostler, on Martina Navratilova
> after an emotional outburst

TOUGHNESS

"The trick against Drysdale is to hit him before he
hits you."

> Orlando Cepeda, on Don Drysdale

"Jimmy Foxx wasn't scouted—he was trapped."

> Lefty Gomez

"The rule was 'No autopsy, no foul.'"

> Stewart Granger, former Cavaliers
> guard, on his rough childhood pickup
> games

"Whenever they gave him the game ball, he ate it."

> Alex Hawkins, on Dick Butkus

"No, but 11 other guys did."
> *Gordie Howe, asked whether he broke*
> *his nose while playing hockey*

"If I was to play against myself and do the things that I did to other people, I'd be mad at me."
> *Maurice Lucas, on his enforcer image*

"The SOB is so mean he'd fucking knock you down in the dugout."
> *Mickey Mantle, on Early Wynn*

"One of those guys who probably even brushes his teeth hard."
> *Gene Mauch, on Brian Downing*

"Rick Dempsey is the kind of guy who would slide headfirst into an iron fence."
> *Lee May*

"Gene Mauch's stare can put you on the disabled list."
> *Tim McCarver*

"He was the only man I ever saw who ran his own interference."
> *Steve Owen, on Bronko Nagurski*

"He's gonna be a great lineman, unless he gets hurt. And if he does, I'd like to have the guy who does it."

Bum Phillips, on Charles Philyaw

"To keep Greg Bingham out of a game, you'd have to cut off his head and then hide it. Just cuttin' off his head wouldn't accomplish anything. He'd find it and try to play anyway."

Bum Phillips

TRADES

"We played him and then we couldn't trade him."

Buzzy Bavasi, on Don Zimmer's play-me-or-trade-me ultimatum

"I hope that when Yogi Berra gets down to talk trades, he'll do just what he did last season—forget about me completely."

Duffy Dyer, discussing trade possibilities

"Being traded is like celebrating your 100th birthday. It might not be the happiest occasion in the world, but consider the alternatives."

Joe Garagiola

"We knew we would have to be a little creative to get anyone to take Ron Cey."

Dallas Green, on offering to pay part of Cey's salary as a trade incentive

"Are you kidding? I haven't the guts for that."

Tom Grieve, on offering weak-hitting Ned Yost in a trade

"I tried growing a beard. That didn't work. I became the player rep. That didn't work. I bought a home. That worked."

Dave Heaverlo, on his attempts to leave the Oakland A's

"I don't know who got me. I dream in black and white, so I couldn't tell what colors the suits were."

Vernon Holland, Bengals tackle, describing a dream in which he was traded

385

"They all want to give me bad players, and I've got enough of those."

> Stan Kasten, GM of the Atlanta Hawks, on why he didn't make any trades

"I'm the only guy on the team with a perforated page in our press guide."

> Brian Kingman, on the trade rumors involving him

"I find that every five years a man has to change his Sox."

> Steve Lyons, on being traded from the Red Sox to the White Sox in 1986 and then back to the Red Sox in 1991

"We didn't want to weaken the rest of the league."

> Joe McDonald, former Mets GM, on why no trades were made on a lousy Mets team

"I wish they'd hurry up and name a general manager, so I can demand to be traded."

> Jawann Oldham, on the Knicks' slow progress in hiring a new GM

"Why do you park on a driveway and drive on a parkway?"

> Larry Andersen, asking another one of his unanswerable questions

"After all the traveling I've done, I demand to be called an international disgrace."

> John Chaney, after being called a national disgrace by Howard Cosell

"This trip must have been planned by the Marquis de Sade Travel Agency."

> Jack Marin, on playing five road games in seven days

"I had more fun and seen more places with less money than if I was Rockefeller."

> Satchel Paige, on playing in the Negro Leagues

"My wife tells me she doesn't care what I do when I'm away as long as I'm not enjoying it."

> Lee Trevino, on being a touring golf pro

"I don't know if we're the oldest battery, but we're certainly the ugliest."

> *Yogi Berra, on Warren Spahn and himself*

"This guy's wife was so ugly he took her on road trips because he couldn't stand to kiss her good-bye."
> *Rocky Bridges*

"That face—it looks like a blocked kick."
> *Joe Garagiola, on Don Zimmer*

"Look, a cab with both doors open."

> *Lefty Gomez, on the very large ears of Cliff Melton*

"I do know one thing for sure. He's got a chance to be a member of the all-ugly club."

> *Grady Hatton, on Fernando Valenzuela*

"Harvy Kuenn's face looks as if it could hold three days of rain."
Tom Lasorda

"The designated gerbil."
Bill Lee, on Don Zimmer

"He throws good, but he's still ugly. He scares the ball to the plate. It'll do anything to get away from him."
Jim Morrison, on Francisco Barrios

"He's so ugly, when you walked by him your pants would wrinkle."
Mickey Rivers, on Dan Napoleon

"He's so ugly that when a fly ball was hit toward him, it would curve away from him."
Mickey Rivers, on Dan Napoleon

"He's so ugly he should have to wear an oxygen mask."
Mickey Rivers, on Cliff Johnson

"He was so ugly as a kid that his parents tied pork chops around his neck so that the dog would play with him."

Lee Trevino, on J. C. Snead

UMPIRES

"Now, what the hell—do you think I'd admit to that?"

Augie Donatelli, asked if he ever made a bad call

"An umpire is like a woman. He makes quick decisions, never reverses them, and doesn't think you're safe when you're out."

Larry Goetz

"Anytime I got the bang-bang play at first base, I called 'em out; it made the game shorter."

Tom Gorman

"It ain't nothing till I call it."

Bill Klem, legendary umpire

"Many fans look upon an umpire as a necessary evil to the luxury of baseball, like the odor that follows an automobile."

Christy Mathewson

"You're expected to be perfect the day you start—and then improve."

Ed Vargo

UNITED STATES

"America has one word that says it all—'You never know.'"

Joaquin Andujar

"Hawaii doesn't win many games in the U.S."

Lee Corso, on why Hawaii doesn't win many games on the mainland

"He looks like an American to me."

Stefan Edberg, asked what he thought of Jim Courier's appearance: a baseball cap and untucked shirt

"America is a wonderful place. You have 15 brands of mayonnaise."

> *Lada Fetisov, wife of former Soviet and current NHL hockey player Viachealav Fetisov*

"Yes. I'm proud to be an American."

> *Steve Foster, Reds pitcher, asked at Canadian customs if he had anything to declare*

"This is the greatest country in America."

> *Bill Petersen*

"I felt like I was punching the American flag."

> *Al Smith, after exchanging punches with 1980 U.S. Olympic hockey hero Jim Craig*

"Not true at all. Vaseline is manufactured right here in the U.S.A."

> *Don Sutton, on accusations that he doctored baseballs with a foreign substance*

"No, but we do have an all-conference guard."
> *Whitman College basketball player,*
> *when asked at the Canadian border if*
> *team members were all Americans*

UTILITY PLAYERS

"I'd feel sorry for him if he were a player."
> *Sal Bando, when designated runner*
> *Herb Washington was cut by the A's*

"I think I hold the record for most games watched, career."
> *Kurt Bevacqua*

"I hate the word utility. It sounds like I work for the electric company."
> *Kurt Bevacqua, on why he would*
> *rather be called a role player than a*
> *utility man*

"It's a great situation for me because I don't have to go out and show my skills too often."

> Dann Bilardello, on being a backup to
> Benito Santiago

"The highlight of your season is taking the team picture, knowing that the trading deadline has passed and you're a part of the club."

> Joe Garagiola, on being a utility
> player

"So far I've played right, left, and first base and I'm Polish. Does that make me a utility pole?"

> Frank Kostro

"Play me or keep me."

> Phil Linz, on being a career utility
> player

"You can't get rich sitting on the bench, but I'm giving it a try."

> Phil Linz

"You're the sultan of squat because you spend so much time on the bench."

Merv Rettenmund, to Larry Brown

"I play many positions—so many positions that I sometimes cannot buy milk for my children because all the money goes for buying gloves."

Chico Ruiz

"I'm the number-one catcher at warming up the pitchers between innings while the other catcher is putting on his gear. I've only had one passed ball doing that all season and not one single runner has stolen on me."

George Thomas

"I bet I'm the only player in the majors who grew up idolizing Ed Spezio."

Alan Trammell, on the former utility infielder

"Every team needs huggers. Those are the guys you sign so you can hug 'em after you win instead of having to hug the guys who play and sweat."

Tommy Vardeman, assistant basketball coach at Centenary College, on backup players

"It's never difficult when you don't do anything."

> *Jim Walewander, asked about the difficulty of going 19 games without getting a chance to hit*

"The coach kept me on the team for morale purposes—I made the other players feel superior."

> *Bud Winters, on his short-lived football career at the University of California*

VACATIONS

"I promised my wife 27 years ago that I would take her to Florida."

> *Lee Corso, on leaving Northern Illinois to coach the Orlando Renegades of the USFL*

"I want to win here, stand on the 18th green and say, 'I'm going to the World Series.'"

> *Larry Nelson, referring to a golf tournament at Disney World*

VANITY

"He wears sunglasses when he goes to X-rated movies."

> *Tom Lasorda, on Steve Garvey's clean-cut image*

VETERANS

"The new criteria for being a veteran is to have been playing when Bryant Gumbel was still covering baseball."

> *Paul Molitor*

VIOLENCE

"It's not good for business if you care for a second whether blood is bubbling from a guy's mouth."

> *Joey Browner, on playing in the NFL*

"I'm just glad it wasn't Machete Night."

Bob Froese, on Rangers fans throwing
plastic mugs on the ice on Mug Night

"Is it normal to wake up in the morning in a sweat because you can't wait to beat another human's guts out?"

Joe Kapp, former NFL quarterback

VOLLEYBALL

"Twenty-two people on the beach who quit playing when the hamburgers are ready."

Steve Timmons, on most people's view
of volleyball players

WALKING

"If you walk backwards, you'll find out that you can go forward and people won't know if you're coming or going."

Casey Stengel

"It's going to be a war out there. I just don't know if we're going to be the U.S. or Kuwait."

Charles Barkley, on the 76ers' prospects in 1992

"The Miami offense can really bomb you. They must get their players from Lebanon or the Middle East somewhere."

Bobby Bowden, on the potent Miami offense

"Any time you want to win a war without shooting bullets, we can draft an NFL tackle and send him to a hostile country in fatigues marked 'small.'"
Mike Ditka

"Pro football is like nuclear warfare. There are no winners—only survivors."
Frank Gifford

"The Cubs won, the Jazz won, BYU was number one, and if World War III had broken out Norway would have won."

> Frank Layden, on 1984, the year of the underdog

"When I was 18 years old and on my belly in Iwo Jima, I used to comfort myself by thinking, 'Boy, am I lucky not having to deal with the pressure of big-time tennis.' "

> Abe Lemons, on John McEnroe's complaints about the pressure of being number one in tennis

"War is hell, but expansion is worse."

> Tom McVie, on his lousy record as an expansion-team coach

"War is the only game in which it doesn't pay to have the home-court advantage."

> Dick Motta

"Now I know why the South lost the Civil War. They must have had the same officials."

> Bum Phillips, after his South team lost to the North in the Senior Bowl

"I went in thinking they couldn't win the war without me. I came out knowing they couldn't win with me."
Bum Phillips, on World War II

WATER

───────────────────────

"Mickey Mantle can hit just as good right-handed as he can left-handed. He's just naturally amphibious."
Yogi Berra

"Where do you buy that stuff?"
Jerry Willard, when told he had to gargle with lukewarm water

WEALTH

───────────────────────

"I hear he's so rich he bought his dog a boy."
Billy Gardner, on Twins' owner Carl Pohlad

"All those kids raised in the slums of Beverly Hills and Newport Beach now see sailing as their way out of the ghetto."

Jay Leno, on what the America's Cup victory meant to southern California

"David's son asked him to buy him a chemistry set, so David went out and bought DuPont."

Pat Williams, on the multimillion-dollar contract signed by NBA Commissioner David Stern

"Shaq's house is in such a great neighborhood the bird feeders have salad bars."

Pat Williams, on the huge contract signed by Shaquille O'Neal

"David is now buying a house in a neighborhood where kids play Little League polo and the Salvation Army band has a string section."

Pat Williams, on David Stern

"You can't worry if it's hot. You can't worry if it's cold. You only worry when you get sick. Because if you don't get well, you die."

Joaquin Andujar, on the weather

"I've seen a lot of bad weather in my times, but if Admiral Byrd were here tonight, he'd turn around and go back."

Rocky Bridges, on a cold night in Buffalo

"It was so muddy, people planted rice at halftime."

Tony Demeo, Mercyhurst College football coach, after a game played on a horrendous field

"I play in the low 80s. If it's any hotter than that, I won't play."

Joe E. Lewis, on golf

"It's a cold business—a cold, cold business. And it's even colder in New England."

> Eugene Lockhart, after being traded from Dallas to New England

"I played as much golf as I could in North Dakota, but summer up there is pretty short. It usually falls on Tuesday."

> Mike Morley, on why he left North Dakota

"When a guy named Noah talks about rain, you listen."

> Yannick Noah fan, overhearing Noah tell someone it wasn't going to rain during a tournament

"Man, it was tough. The wind was blowing about 100 degrees."

> Mickey Rivers, on weather conditions at a game

"I'm from Florida so I'm used to it. Actually, the climaxes are about the same."

> Mickey Rivers, on the Texas heat

404

"It's so cold out there, I saw a dog chasing a cat and they were both walking."

Mickey Rivers, on a 48-degree game

"I wouldn't say it's cold, but every year Winnipeg's athlete of the year is an ice fisherman."

Dale Tallon

WEDDINGS

"If Americans throw rice at weddings, do Chinese throw hot dogs?"

Larry Andersen, asking another one of his unanswerable questions

"I have a daughter getting married. If we don't make the playoffs, she'll have to elope."

Dick Jamieson, Cardinals' running-back coach

"My wife wanted a big diamond."

Mookie Wilson, on why he got married in a ballpark

"He's so thin the 76ers' don't bother to take him on the road—they just fax him from town to town."

Woody Allen, on Manute Bol

"After games, he can be a sumo wrestler."

Mark Bolen, Terry Forster's agent, on why his client wanted to play in Japan

"We put him on the Cambridge diet, and he ate half of Cambridge."

Ed Croke, Giants PR director, on Leonard Marshall

"Like they say: It ain't over till the fat guy swings."

Darren Daulton, on teammate John Kruk

"We all get heavier as we get older because there's a lot more information in our heads—our heads weigh more."

Vlade Divac, explaining how he gained 15 pounds in the off-season

"The only man who could pitch in 90-degree weather and still gain weight."
> Harry Dorish, on Jack Lamabe

"Don't you know it's illegal to let two men bat at the same time?"
> Leo Durocher, on 250-pound Fat Fothergill

"I'm going to eat hamburgers and cheeseburgers. I'm going to belly bump him all over the ring."
> George Foreman, on how he was going to fight Evander Holyfield

"A waist is a terrible thing to mind."
> Terry Forster

"I thought he'd been at the beach all summer—he still had his inner tube around his stomach."
> Billy Gardner, on Rich Yett

"They're both trying to make the final fork."
> Sam Goldaper, watching heavyweights Rick Majerus and Frank Layden eat their way through a basketball banquet

"I almost made people forget Lefty Gomez."

Lefty Gomez, urged to gain weight in the off-season so that he would make people forget Lefty Grove

"I have to jump around in the shower to get wet."

Bruce Kison, on being 6′4″, 175 pounds

"It looks like the same thing George Scott wore around his waist when he was trying to lose weight."

Bill Lee, on the orange roof in Montreal's Olympic Stadium

"If I'm winning, I'm roly-poly or chubby; if I'm losing I'm fat or slobby."

Mickey Lolich

"When I'm out there pitching a Saturday game that is nationally televised, there is a fat guy in front of the set at home in his T-shirt and shorts. He looks at me and says, 'See Mabel, that guy's fat just like me. Now get me another beer, will ya?'"

Mickey Lolich

"You could house 20 homeless families in them."
Rick Majerus, former heavyset college
basketball coach, on his sweaters

"Rick Majerus losing 20 pounds is like the Queen Mary losing a deck chair."
Al McGuire

"In the off-season he got a job as a left-field foul line in a slow-pitch softball league."
Ed Nottles, on pitcher Chris Codiroli

"He went to bed as a 231-pound world champion and woke up as a 270-pound parade float."
Scott Ostler, on Buster Douglas

"Even when I was little, I was big."
William "Refrigerator" Perry

"It takes a lot of guts to play this game, and by looking at Billy Casper, you can tell he certainly has a lot of guts."
Gary Player

"I've reserved three seats for you at my show tonight. One for you, one for your wife, and one for your stomach."

> *Don Rickles, to Don Zimmer*

"I'll guarantee that he had chocolate syrup in the bottle."

> *Mike Scioscia, on the formerly heavy Tom Lasorda doing a Diet Coke commercial*

"The only spread that Jimmy the Greek is an expert on is the one under his belt."

> *Art Spander*

"So what? I run wind sprints around the Fridge."

> *Matt Suhey, after hearing that Walter Payton stayed in shape by running up and down hills*

"I don't need a chest protector. I need a bra."

> *Gus Triandos, on being a fat catcher at an old-timers' game*

"We got him eating the seven basic food groups, and now there are only three left."

Pat Williams, on Stanley Roberts

"Stanley's chosen his burial site: Montana."

Pat Williams, on Stanley Roberts

"You know the old saying 'No man is an island?' Stanley comes close."

Pat Williams, on Stanley Roberts

"He could be the 1991 poster boy for jelly doughnuts. When he was here, we had to remove an obstruction from his throat. It was a pizza."

Pat Williams, on—guess who?

"I can't use those fat jokes anymore—Stanley has turned over a new chin."

Pat Williams, on Stanley Roberts when his weight dropped under 300 pounds

"McDonald's and Wendy's are suing Stanley for non-support."

Pat Williams, on the new, skinnier Stanley Roberts

"He's so skinny his pajamas have only one pinstripe."

Pat Williams, on Manute Bol

"He looks like he went to the blood bank and forgot to say 'when.' "

Pat Williams, on Bol

WIMBLEDON

"New Yorkers love it when you spill your guts out there. You spill your guts at Wimbledon, they make you stop and clean it up."

Jimmy Connors, comparing Wimbledon to the U.S. Open

WIMPS

"If they did, I'd stomp 'em and do a pirouette on their head."

Ken Avery, former NFL football player, on being asked what he would do if he were called a sissy for practicing ballet

"You could send Inge Hammarstrom into the corner with six eggs in his pocket and he wouldn't break any of them."

>*Harold Ballard, on the timid play of the former Toronto Maple Leaf*

"If the game becomes more namby-pamby, they may have to put the ball on a batting tee."

>*Don Drysdale, on baseball*

"Why should a guy with a half-million dollar contract want to have blood dripping down his face or sweat or play with bruises? Hell, they won't even play with bruised feelings now."

>*Bobby Hull, on the state of pro sports*

"If I had as many singles as Pete Rose, I'd have worn a dress."

>*Mickey Mantle*

"For a guy 6'8", he's got the softest bat I've ever seen, and for George Steinbrenner to give him $23 million—he must be losing his horsefeathers."

>*Billy Martin, on Dave Winfield*

"If the meek are going to inherit the earth, our offensive linemen are going to be land barons."

Bill Muir, on the SMU offensive line

"An NFL game today is like a golf tournament in which you play your way up to the green and find a guy from Brazil standing there to do the putting for you."

Norm Pollum, Buffalo Bills' director of scouting

"What makes you think God loves wimps?"

David Robinson, asked if being a born-again Christian would make him a weaker player

"Red is kind of a wimpy color. Maybe next year they'll make us wear little flowers on our jerseys, up around the shoulder pads. And then they can have Big Bird on the side of our pants to make the kids happy."

Fred Smerlas, on the Bills' changing from white to red football helmets

"Show me a guy who's afraid to look bad, and I'll show you a guy you can beat every time."

Lou Brock

"When you win, you're an old pro. When you lose, you're an old man."

Charlie Connerly

"Winning is the name of the game. The more you win, the less you get fired."

Bep Guidolin, former Bruins' coach

"At USC, you're expected to be great. Not good—great! We win the Liberty Bowl last year, and the trophy doesn't even make the front room."

Paul Hackett, former USC quarterback coach

"Winning is like shaving—you do it every day or you wind up looking like a bum."

Jack Kemp

"The will to win is not nearly as important as the will to prepare to win."

Bobby Knight

"The secret to keep winning streaks going is to maximize the victories while at the same time minimizing the defeats."

John Lowenstein

"It's just like you all expected—Edberg, Lendl, McEnroe, and Becker."

Patrick McEnroe, on making the semis of the Australian Open

"Once you start keeping score, winning's the bottom line. It's the American concept. If not, it's like playing your grandmother, and even then you try to win— unless she has a lot of money and you want to get some of it."

Al McGuire

"The only time Jim didn't run up the score was 27 years ago when he took the SAT."

Jim Nantz, on Dallas Cowboys coach Jim Johnson

"The longer you play, the better chance the better player has of winning."

Jack Nicklaus

"When you win, you eat better, sleep better, and your wife looks like Gina Lollabrigida."

Johnny Pesky

"It's not how many you win that's important; it's how many you show up for."

Barclay Plager

"Any time you put together a two-game winning streak, they give you a trophy."

Bill Sudek, Case Western Reserve basketball coach, on preseason tournaments

"Never change a winning game; always change a losing one."

Bill Tilden

"Very simple. Nothing will work unless you do."

John Wooden, on his secret of winning

"I know a baseball star who wouldn't report the theft of his wife's credit cards because the thief spends less than she does."

Joe Garagiola

"No need to worry about my arm. I carried my wife's bag through the airport."

Jay Howell, responding to questions about having a sore arm

"It's like your wife. If you want something from her, you butter her up."

Cliff Johnson, on why he kisses his bat in pressure situations

"I'd let my wife support me. I'd sit on a couch in a torn T-shirt, drink beer, and watch Bob Newhart on TV."

Kurt Nimphius, on what he would do if he didn't play basketball

"We met at Purdue. She was a drum majorette, sang with a band, had her own radio show, gave baton lessons, and was a brilliant student. She was definitely a number-one draft choice."

Hank Stram, describing his wife

"I'm the only man alive whose wife approves of him going around with fast women."

Ed Temple, women's track coach, Tennessee State

"It's one thing to hear about it from your coach, but when your wife tells you it stinks, you tend to work on it."

Orlando Woolridge, on how he improved his free-throw shooting

WOMEN

"I thought the only thing he did in the minors was chase broads. When did you have time to learn how to pitch?"

Steve Barber, on Bo Belinsky

"Give me golf clubs, fresh air, and a beautiful partner, and you can keep my golf clubs and the fresh air."
Jack Benny

"I don't think American girls like to house clean. I tried American girls. They talk too much."
Manute Bol, on why he married a woman from his native country, Sudan

"I've dated girls who were far better looking than the quality of the girls who should be going out with me."
Cris Collinsworth, on the advantages of being an NFL player

"Mitch found God in spring training. Then every night he went looking for a goddess."
Len Dykstra, on former teammate Kevin Mitchell

"You mean it was OK before this?"
Jack Hamilton, after Mets' manager Wes Westrum said that from now on there would be no women in the hotel rooms (as told by Ron Swoboda)

"I would still rather score a touchdown than make love to the prettiest girl in the U.S."

Paul Hornung

"In the daytime, you sat in the dugout and talked about women. At night you went out with women and talked about baseball."

Waite Hoyt, on baseball in the old days

"When we won the league championship, all the married guys on the club had to thank their wives for putting up with all the stress and strain all season. I had to thank all the single broads in New York."

Joe Namath

"It's no coincidence that female interest in the sport of baseball has increased greatly since the ballplayers swapped those wonderful old-time baggy flannel uniforms for leotards."

Mike Royko

"Victories. People don't even know what ERA means except those who follow Alan Alda around."

Dave Stewart, asked if he would rather lead the league in victories or ERA

"The time-outs smell a lot better."

Butch van Breda Kolff, on why he liked coaching a female basketball team better than a male team

WORLD SERIES

"It's never happened in the World Series competition, and it still hasn't."

Yogi Berra, on Don Larsen's perfect game

"When we played, World Series checks meant something. Now all they do is screw up your taxes."
Don Drysdale

"Clean living and a fast outfield."

Lefty Gomez, explaining why he had such a great World Series record

"Anybody who says he isn't nervous or excited in a World Series is either crazy or a liar."
Rogers Hornsby

422

"You have the right to suffer. You have the right to feel pain. If you wish to have an attorney present, I'll hurt him too."

> *Big Boss Man, professional wrestler who wears a police uniform and goes around reading each opponent his rights*

"I believe that professional wrestling is clean and everything else in the world is fixed."
> *Frank Deford*

"I don't know what it is, but I can't look at Hulk Hogan and believe that he's the end result of millions and millions of years of evolution."
> *Jim Murray*

WRITING

"Ransom notes."

> *Alex Karras, offering his opinion on the most profitable type of writing*

"The profession of book writing makes horseracing seem like a solid, stable business."

> *John Steinbeck*

YMCA

"We did have three go to the YMCA."

> *Abe Lemons, asked if any of his players from Oklahoma State made it to the NBA*

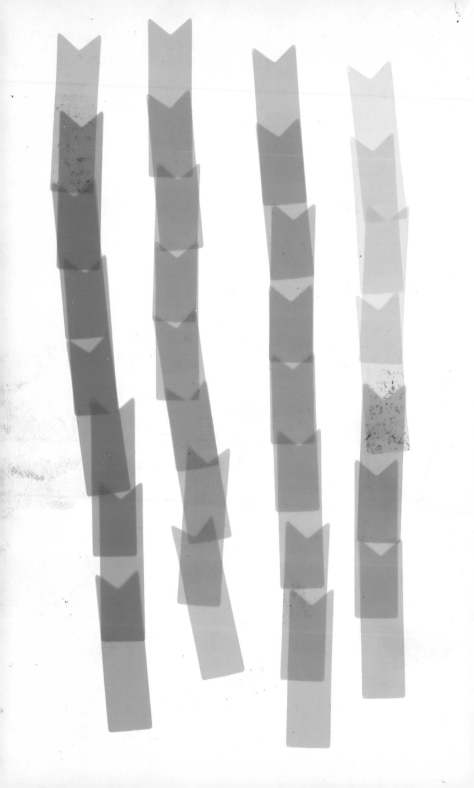